Psychologists in the Criminal Justice System

Stanley L. Brodsky

UNIVERSITY OF ILLINOIS PRESS
Urbana   Chicago   London

77641

Illini Books edition, 1973
By permission from the American Association of Correctional Psychologists
© 1972 by the American Association of Correctional Psychologists
Manufactured in the United States of America
Library of Congress Catalog Card No. 72-87472
ISBN 0-252-00432-9

This report and the background conferences were partially supported by Grant
#54-0381 from the Youth Development and Delinquency Prevention Administration,
with joint sponsorship by the National Institute of Mental Health and the Law Enforcement Assistance Administration.

The opinions expressed herein are the views of the author and contributors, and
are not intended to reflect the official position of the American Association of Correctional Psychologists, the National Institute of Mental Health, the Youth Development and Delinquency Prevention Administration, the Law Enforcement Assistance
Administration, or any organization or agency associated with this project.

Table
of Contents

77641

Table of Contents

Table of Contents

Contributors

There were two ways, often overlapping, in which individuals were active in developing this document. One route was the authoring of a chapter. The other was participation in one of the background conferences. While the latter contributors are not identified by personal credits throughout the text, their knowledge and ideas were integrated into many of the chapters. The enthusiasm and generosity of all these contributors are gratefully acknowledged.

AUTHORS OF CHAPTERS

David L. Bazelon, Judge, U.S. Court of Appeals, Washington, D.C.
Lawrence A. Bennett, California Department of Corrections, Sacramento
Stanley L. Brodsky, University of Alabama
Bertram S. Brown, Director, National Institute of Mental Health
Don M. Gottfredson, National Council on Crime and Delinquency,
    Davis California
Gilbert Ingram, Federal Correctional Institution, Tallahassee, Florida
Lorrin M. Koran, National Institute of Mental Health
Richard A. McGee, American Justice Institute, Sacramento, California
Edwin I. Megargee, Florida State University
Charles D. Spielberger, Florida State University
David Twain, City College of New York
Marguerite Q. Warren, Center for Differential Treatment, Sacramento

x **PARTICIPANTS IN LAKE WALES CONFERENCE
OR FOLLOW-UP MEETINGS**

David L. Bazelon, Judge, U.S. Court of Appeals, Washington, D.C.
Hobart M. Banks, California Department of Corrections, Sacramento
Lawrence A. Bennett, California Department of Corrections, Sacramento
Vincent Biasi, Staten Island, New York
Alan Boneau, American Psychological Association
Terry Brelje, Psychiatric Division, Illinois Department of Corrections
Stanley L. Brodsky, University of Alabama
Robert Callahan, National Institute of Mental Health
Margaret Clay, Mental Health Research Institute, University of Michigan
John P. Conrad, National Institute of Law Enforcement and Criminal
    Justice
Robert Fosen, New York Department of Correctional Services
Raymond Fowler, University of Alabama
John S. Friedman, The American Foundation, Philadelphia
Don M. Gottfredson, National Council on Crime and Delinquency,
    Davis, California
Arnold J. Hopkins, American Bar Association
Charles L. Horn, Research and Treatment Center, Gainesville, Florida
George Howard, Center for Differential Treatment, Sacramento
Gilbert Ingram, Federal Correctional Institution, Tallahassee, Florida
Arthur Kandel, Patuxent Institution, Jessup, Maryland
Thomas C. Kowalski, Ohio Reformatory for Women, Marysville
Frank Lee, Middle Tennessee State University, Murfreesboro
Robert B. Levinson, Federal Bureau of Prisons, Washington, D.C.
William H. Lyle, Public Health Service Hospital, New Orleans, Louisiana
Roslyn McDonald, New York Division for Youth
Edwin I. Megargee, Florida State University
Sherman Nelson, National Institute of Mental Health
Ronald Nuehring, Florida State University
Asher R. Pacht, Wisconsin Division of Corrections
Clarence Schrag, University of Washington, Seattle
Stanley F. Schneider, National Institute of Mental Health
Robert E. Schulman, The Menninger Foundation, Topeka, Kansas
Gottlieb C. Simon, American Psychological Association
Mitchell Silverman, University of South Florida
David Twain, City College of New York
Marguerite Q. Warren, Center for Differential Treatment, Sacramento
George Weber, National Institute of Mental Health

Introduction

The purpose of this report is to describe what psychologists do in justice systems, what they should be doing, and what knowledge and methods are necessary. This document attempts to compile and synthesize existing activities of psychologists concerned with law violation, social deviance and justice. Next, it seeks to identify societal and justice system needs and problems that are appropriate for active participation of psychologists. This step takes the form of attempting to legitimize worthwhile functions that are not widespread, and of offering policy suggestions for psychological research and services. Finally, it indicates a number of ways to attain these objectives. The methods range from developments in graduate education to specific examples of psychologists introducing public policy and justice system changes.

The reader is requested to bear with an occasional disciplinary myopia. This document becomes "psychology-centric," all too often, when practices are discussed as if no other profession or discipline could perform them. It is not so. In most cases, there is a functional overlap of psychology with other disciplines and professions, rather than the subject matter being a proprietary interest of psychology. The predominant content concerns what psychologists have been doing and the roles they are assuming.

It should be understood that crime is a legal artifact. When the words "criminal," "delinquent," or "offender" are used, this indicates an acceptance of a legal definition. When omission of the use of "offender," "criminal,"

2   etc., throughout the monograph was considered, the language proved to be awkward. "Criminal" and other labels have been used, but have not been automatically assumed to be behavioral entities.

Just as convicted persons cannot be behaviorally grouped as "criminal," in a related sense justice systems and agencies are not all alike. The variations among law enforcement agencies, or among correctional institutions, are great and the differing objectives, functions and character of justice agencies yield a myriad of conflicting activities and models. Thus the frequent statements about justice agencies have this inherent limitation.

The intended audiences for this document are, first, psychologists and students who are active or interested in law and justice, and, secondly, administrators in justice agencies and members of other disciplines, with interest in psychological processes related to justice. It is intended to provide a common base of knowledge and information for these groups. It further seeks to mobilize psychologists and administrators toward broader, potentially more effective collaborative activities, and to increase awareness of new developments in utilizing psychological skills and knowledge.

The material in this report developed from a series of conferences. In January, 1972, 30 psychologists, sociologists, attorneys and justice agency administrators gathered for three days at Lake Wales, Florida. Four position papers on psychology and justice had been commissioned prior to this meeting. The authors and topics of the position papers were:

David Twain, *Roles and Functions of Psychology in the Criminal Justice System*
Charles D. Spielberger, Edwin I. Megargee, and Gilbert L. Ingram, *Graduate Education in Psychology Related to the Problems of Crime, Delinquency and Corrections.*
Richard A. McGee and Lawrence A. Bennett, *Needs for and Uses of Psychological Services in the Criminal Justice System from the Point of View of the Administrator*
Don Gottfredson, *Five Challenges to Correctional Psychology*

All four of these were modified by the conference and appear as chapters in their revised forms.

A special note should be made of the evolution of the Richard McGee/Lawrence Bennett position paper into its present form. Since some of their suggestions coincided with the content of other chapters, their recommendations and lists of functions were distilled and subsequently edited to supplement the contents of five chapters. This position paper included a comprehensive distribution of criminal justice system needs as perceived not only by McGee and Bennett, but also by a number of criminal justice administrators. The contributions of the following persons to the McGee-Bennett paper are

Allen F. Breed
Milton Burdman
Michael Canlis
Norman A. Carlson
Winslow Christian
Allen Cook
Bertram S. Griggs
Richard F. C. Hyden
Eleanor W. Hiller
Delmar Huebner
Laurence M. Hyde, Jr.
Paul W. Keve

Robert Kingsley
William J. Kinney
Kenneth E. Kirkpatrick
Gene S. Muehleisen
Vincent O'Leary
John W. Oliver
Thomas G. Pinnock
Sanger B. Powers
Milton G. Rector
George J. Reed
John A. Wallace

Judge David L. Bazelon's paper, presented to the Lake Wales conference, appears as Appendix A. While excerpts of it have been widely reported by the news services, the present document is the first publication of his complete text. The accompanying comments in Appendix B by psychiatrists Lorrin Koran and Bertram Brown, represent an alternate view of psychologists in justice agencies, from the perspective of an outside profession.

Three one-day conferences followed the Lake Wales meeting. The five or six persons gathered at each of these meetings organized and synthesized the material discussed in Florida. Decisions for inclusion of additional chapters were made in those meetings, including the request of Marguerite Warren to prepare a chapter on the psychologist as action researcher. Finally, the continuing interchange of ideas between many of the conference participants became part of the content of this final report.

This project and report would not have been possible without the support of the Youth Development and Delinquency Prevention Administration, the Law Enforcement Assistance Administration and the National Institute of Mental Health. Arthur Kandel and Thomas Kowalski were instrumental in early discussion and creation of this project. Michael Dana, John Conrad, and Saleem Shah, as representatives of the federal sponsoring agencies, were sources of consistent good advice and guidance.

Several people will recognize, within the text, the selective pirating of their ideas and suggestions. No one has had the Jolly Roger raised near him more than Robert Levinson. In addition, he has given painstaking and thorough critiques of the whole work, undoubtedly wielding the fastest blue pencil in the East.

There are many other people and organizations that have contributed. The American Foundation provided the use of the Pinewood Estate and Mountain Lake Sanctuary at Lake Wales, which gave the conference partic-

4 ipants a serene and relaxing setting in which to work.

There were several participants who read draft copies of chapters and shared their impressions. Appreciation for these efforts is extended to Robert Schulman, James Olsson, Asher Pacht and Hobart Banks. Charles Horn and Jay Friedman provided both invaluable suggestions and good role models in the discussions of social activism and commitments. Saleem Shah has contributed generously to the development of the topics of dangerousness and social policy in the text.

As the project progressed, Diane Leach became a colleague as well as a secretary and offered valuable help in this dual role. Mittie Parish Schindler requires special mention. Her overall rewriting, editorial assistance, and personal involvement in the project, produced a more precise and readable manuscript. To Jackie Goepfert, Margaret Camarato, Darnecea Moultrie, and Stephanie Holmes, I am indebted for secretarial work performed under conditions of perpetually unreasonable deadlines.

This report may reflect another of those ventures in which the final product is far less than the input and discussions that led up to it. Certainly, the informal experience, meetings, and discussions were unusually worthwhile for those involved. It is hoped that the conference and this report will serve as a starting point for more professional activities and scientific interest in psychology and justice. It is intended to be a point along the path to answering the questions: What are psychologists doing in this area? Where are they going? And how do they get there?

Psychologists in
Criminal Justice Systems:
Looking Back
and Looking Around

LOOKING BACK

From Criminal Anthropology to Scientific Psychology

As the second half of the nineteenth century unfolded, both criminology and psychology were awakening as major disciplines. Penal reform was a popular theme. Police were becoming accepted and professionalized. An Italian physician named Lombroso was pioneering scientific criminology by studying the physical measurements of criminals. And the science of psychology was slowly maturing in laboratories in Germany.

William James established the first psychological laboratory in the United States, at Harvard in the late 19th century, then brought Hugo Munsterberg from Freiburg, Germany to direct it and to teach psychology. Munsterberg became interested in applying psychology to industry and to the law. His book *On the Witness Stand* (1907) identified many psychological processes influencing witnesses with respect to their perception and recollection. Munsterberg's work has persisted as a frame of reference for major investigations of testimony (Kolasa, 1972).

Lombroso and the other criminal anthropologists of the continent promoted the scientific study of crime in the English-speaking nations. In England, in 1883, Francis Galton attributed criminality to intrinsic, hereditary, fixed factors, demonstrated both by behavior and anthropometric studies (Murphy, 1949). In the same Darwinian vein, Havelock Ellis' book *The*

6 *Criminal,* published in 1890, dealt largely with criminality as related to anthropological measurements, and stimulated studies in individual differences among offenders (Hearnshaw, 1964). However, within 30 years, much of the interest in criminal anthropology had subsided. In his study, *The English Convict,* which appeared in 1913, Charles Goring found no differences in physical measurements between samples of 3,000 convicts and 3,000 college students (Hearnshaw, 1964). Psychological research reports about criminality were becoming commonplace; the sprouts of scientific study and psychological theorizing about criminality were flourishing.

Criminality and Applied Psychology

The turn of the century was marked by the emergence of applied as well as scientific psychology. In 1896, Lightner Witmer invented the term "clinical psychology" and opened the first psychological clinic. Located at the University of Pennsylvania, his clinic extended psycho-educational services to school children (Misiak & Sexton, 1966). In a survey taken 18 years later, 26 such clinics, concerned with intellectual development and school performance of school pupils, had been established.

When William Healy established the Juvenile Psychopathic Institute in Chicago in 1909, the psychological clinic became attached to another newly conceived service facility, the juvenile court. Healy's institute acted as advisor to the Judge of the Juvenile Court of Chicago, made recommendations, and offered treatment to juveniles under the court's jurisdiction. While the criminal anthropologists had concentrated on physical measurements and species regressiveness of the criminal, and while Witmer had emphasized intellectual development and adjustment, Healy preached and practiced a psychodynamic approach. He was concerned with emotional functioning, social pathology and general questions of dishonesty and maladjustment (Healy, 1915; Healy & Healy, 1915; Healy, Bronner, Baylor, & Murphy, 1929).

Within a discipline, the same scientific knowledge often makes simultaneous but independent appearances. Thus, at the same time Healy was working with Chicago delinquents, Cyril Burt was testing British criminals as part of his work with the London County Council. Burt's 1925 book *The Young Delinquent,* like Healy's writings, indicated that crime was caused by multiple, dynamic determinants. Burt took the position that criminality was primarily a psychological phenomenon, and that social, genetic and physical factors also contributed to its development (Hearnshaw, 1964).

During World War I, psychological services were applied on a wider scale than ever before. Millions of men were tested and classified, then selected or rejected for military duty on the basis of newly developed intelligence tests and psychiatric rating scales. On the coattails of this publicized wartime success, psychologists and many other testers rode into almost every aspect of American life. Among these new spheres of influence was the justice agency. Thus, when the first prison classification program in the nation was established in New Jersey in 1918, psychologists developed it and controlled it throughout the state (Barnes & Teeters, 1959).

As psychoanalysis was expanded as a theory and treatment method in the early 20th century, it provided a basis for understanding and dealing with virtually all deviant behaviors. For example, criminality was interpreted through psychoanalytic principles in Alexander and Staub's (1931) *The Criminal, the Judge, and the Public.* The neurotic criminal was classified as a major type; such offenders were seen as being propelled to their criminal acts by unconsciously motivated aggression and guilt.

The subsequent steps in applying psychology to offenders and justice agencies may be traced through several paths. The more important events in these developments include organized longitudinal research on offender characteristics and later recidivism (Glueck & Glueck, 1930), intensive case studies of offenders (Karpman, 1933), the integration of professional knowledge about psychology and offenders (Lindner & Seliger, 1947), and coping with the stigma of psychologists working in justice agencies (Corsini, 1945; Corsini & Miller, 1954).

This brief review has indicated some influential persons, turning points, and qualitative advances in the development of criminal psychology. The next questions are: To what extent do psychologists identify law-violation and justice problems as their area of interest? How did (and does) psychology's activities in research and practice compare to those of other disciplines?

Publications and Research

The number of publications reported in the two major psychology abstracting journals from 1894 through 1970 are presented in Table 1. In the *Psychological Index* the number of crime-related articles ranged from 189 in the five-year period, 1901-1905, up to 664 for the period, 1926-1930. The percentage of articles that were crime-related varied from 1.3% to 2.7% of total articles abstracted. These data represent, for the most part, publications in French and German, with up to 90% of the articles appearing in only one of these languages. Furthermore the *Psychological Index* results do not exclusively reflect crime studies. From 1911-1935, degeneracy, prostitution and suicide were considered part of criminology and delinquency. While the definition of crime is elusive, this inclusion is overly broad and does not permit total acceptance of this information. The early classification of criminology under the heading of Race Pathology was not a sign of scientific bigotry or racism, but rather a continuation of the anthropological, Darwinian view of criminality as inborn and determined.

The *Psychological Abstracts*, concerned primarily with articles written in English, was similarly examined. It was found that the percentage of crime-related publications generally decreased after the inception of *Psych-*

Incidence of Crime-Related Publications in the *Psychological Index,*
1894-1935, and in the *Psychological Abstracts,* 1927 - 1970

Psychological Index:

Years	Listings Under "Criminology"[a]	Total Articles	% Criminology
1894-95	75	2,706	2.7
1896-1900	306	12,498	2.4
1901-05	189	13,907	1.3
1906-10	215	15,927	1.3
1911-15	309	14,911	2.1
1916-20	191	11,973	1.6
1921-25	375	18,273	2.1
1926-30	664	29,754	2.2
1931-35	562	30,882	1.8
Totals	**2,886**	**150,831**	**1.9**

Psychological Abstracts:

Listings[b]

Years	Crime	Delinquency	Prisoners	Total Crime Related	Total Articles	% Crime Related	% of 1931-35 Base
1927-30	263	126	65	454	16,643	2.7	—
1931-35	466	247	111	824	28,523	2.9	100
1936-40	530	321	46	897	31,650	2.8	109
1941-45	324	390	47	761	22,306	3.4	92
1946-50	330	307	102	739	28,309	2.6	90
1951-55	273	384	80	737	41,934	1.8	90
1956-60	220	510	137	867	43,490	2.0	105
1961-65	198	417	93	708	50,720	1.4	86
1966-70	528	639	198	1,365	88,552	1.5	166
Totals	**3,068**	**3,280**	**874**	**7,222**	**347,061**	**2.1**	

[a]From 1900 to 1910 Criminology was a subheading under "RACE PATHOLOGY."
The other subheading was "DEGENERATION and SEX PATHOLOGY." From 1911 to
1935 these references were drawn from the single heading of "DEGENERACY,
PROSTITUTION, CRIMINOLOGY, SUICIDE, and DELINQUENCY."
[b]There were also a small number of listings under the headings "LAW" and
"ANTISOCIAL BEHAVIOR," which are not included here.

logical Abstracts. Until 1950, the number of crime-related articles never constituted less than 2.5% of total publications. In the subsequent five-year periods from 1951 through 1970, the number was never higher than 2.0% and dropped to the lowest levels in this half-century during 1961-1970. The absolute number of crime-related articles stayed fairly constant from 1931 through 1965, while the publication rate for all of psychology rose approximately 100%. In the 1966-1970 period, for the first time, the rate of increase of publications in this area kept pace with the overall increase rate in American psychology.

What do these figures mean? They give us no information about the quality of research or reports, since the number of publications is not a barometer of impact or progress. However, they do reflect the extent of psychologists' investment of time and interest in the offender and justice systems. Thus, it appears that for the last 50 years, a proportionately decreasing amount of interest and priority was assigned by American psychologists to writing about criminological and justice content areas.

A comparative estimate of the amount of research conducted in the different behavioral sciences was obtained by examining the dissertations in crime and law enforcement published by University Microfilms (1972) during the period, 1938-1970. A sample, consisting of the alphabetically first 144 of the more than 700 listed dissertation topics, was studied and the titles were classified by apparent disciplinary affiliation. Twenty-five per cent were clearly conducted by psychologists; they dealt with testing, psychotherapy, or topics associated with psychological technical proficiency (e.g., A comparison of the individual Rorschach method and the group discussion Rorschach method as a diagnostic device with delinquent adolescent boys). The 8% that were conducted in schools of education for the EdD degree, were primarily psychological in nature. Twenty-eight per cent were apparently sociological, and 20% were of uncertain disciplinary origin. The remainder were distributed among social work, criminology, public administration, government, and other social or behavioral science disciplines. In the case of a few of the psychology dissertations, the interest in offenders or in the law enforcement process was secondary to some discipline-specific issue. However, for the largest number, the topics were oriented to justice problems. Thus, more dissertations dealing with offenders and with justice agencies and systems were completed by psychologists than by other behavioral scientists. And there is no reason to believe that this pattern is independent of the full array of criminological research projects.

LOOKING AROUND

Grants

An important, current source of information about criminal justice

10   research is the extent of support provided by federal funding agencies. Table 2 shows the proportion of support given to psychologists in research and training grants and in fellowships by the Center for the Studies of Crime and Delinquency of the National Institute of Mental Health (NIMH). Just under half of the research grants active in fiscal year (FY) 1972 had psychologists as principal investigators. The majority of the remaining principal investigators were sociologists. Only 2 of 52 training grants went to psychologists. However, this category represented a major financial source for Social Work-Corrections programs and most NIMH support for psychology graduate programs comes from another branch of NIMH. Overall, 28% of the recipients were psychologists, a figure that corresponds closely to the proportion of crime and law enforcement dissertations written by psychologists.

Psychologists in Justice Agencies and Activities
    The number of psychologists working in justice settings, or considering crime and justice as a specialty area, is difficult to ascertain. In 1968, the American Psychological Association (APA) mailed a social-problem questionnaire to its members and received 14,500 replies. Of these, 55 psychologists considered themselves qualified to consult or advise with government bodies or private organizations in the area of law enforcement (which was the only questionnaire category relevant to justice activities). In the 1970 National Register of Scientific and Technical Personnel, Forensic Psychology was listed. Only 42 psychologists of over 26,000 respondents checked this as their employment or scientific specialty. These figures appear to be underestimates of the number of psychologists interested in justice and offenders. This is due to the limitations of the questionnaire items, to the number of non-APA psychologists employed in the justice agencies, and to the number of independent psychological associations concerned with law, justice and corrections.
    Between the American Psychology-Law Society, the International Academy of Forensic Psychology, and the American Association of Correctional Psychologists, about 800 psychologist-members identify themselves as having substantial interest in law, justice, or corrections. Since 1967, APA has had a Task Force on Crime, Delinquency, and Social Disorders and, since 1970, a Task Force on Standards for Service Facilities. The APA Division of Psychological Aspects of Disability has an *ad hoc* Committee on the Public Offender. Division 9, the Society for the Psychological Study of Social Issues (SPSSI), has several active committees, and probably represents the highest level of organized interest in APA. The number of APA convention programs presented in crime, law enforcement and justice has risen from 3 to 4 annually in the mid 1960's to over 20 annually in the early 1970's. Offender and justice psychologists do seem to be alive and well and occasionally in residence at the American Psychological Association.

TABLE 2
NIMH Research and Training Grants and Fellowships Funded by the Center for Studies of Crime and Delinquency[a]

Category	Psychologist as Principal Investigator	Total Awarded
RESEARCH GRANTS		
Active FY 1972	26	55
Prior to FY 1972	12	31
RESEARCH CONTRACTS	1	3
TRAINING GRANTS		
Active FY 1972	2	52
Prior to FY 1972	2	10
FELLOWSHIPS		
Active FY 1972	4	16
Prior to FY 1972	0	5
SUM OF CATEGORIES	47 (28%)	171

[a]Saleem Shah, Chief of the Center for Studies of Crime and Delinquency, generously provided the project summaries on which this information is based.

Chapter 1

The pattern of small societies with diffuse undirected functioning exists in other mental health professions and behavioral sciences with specialties in justice. Similarly they have not formed strong voices or organizations either within their own professional societies or across disciplines. If unified and influential voices are to be raised from these perspectives, then perhaps it is time to bring these diverse behavioral scientists together in order to integrate knowledge and achieve common objectives.

Justice Agencies and Departments

Over 80 justice-focused academic departments and public service and private agencies employ behavioral scientists and mental health professionals. The appearance of these diverse multidisciplinary units is a relatively new phenomenon. Their goals vary, encompassing education, research, direct clinical service, and occasionally, profit making.

These multidisciplinary organizations are important for several reasons. They represent channels for input of psychological and other behavioral science knowledge, without the limitations and bureaucratic difficulties often found in traditional direct service agencies. Since these centers are growing rapidly in number and influence, they probably will take on even more significant and influential functions in the future. They represent a source of professional stimulation that is good for the discipline of psychology as well as the justice field. While supplying an additional area of employment for psychologists, they also train new scientists and professionals and send better equipped practitioners into direct service agencies. They often provide educational experiences for large numbers of pre-service and in-service justice system personnel, and thus may influence activities on a wide scale. And finally, when organizations must compete for funding, and necessarily be subjected to evaluation, psychologists become increasingly sensitive to their own program's relative adequacy. Competition, then, instills in the psychologist a sense of accountability that raises the standards of professional competency.

SUMMARY

As psychology developed in the twentieth century, its knowledge and skills in professional human services were applied to a variety of justice problems and settings. The scientific applications of psychology were initially seen with skepticism at the turn of the century, but have assumed a clear role in the overall justice research picture. Some samplings of research information among the behavioral sciences suggest that about 25-30% of criminally related behavioral science research is carried out by psychologists or is primarily psychological in nature. Among psychologists this currently represents about 1.5% of ongoing research, as measured by quantity of publications. This decline in research in justice problems as a specialty area is just beginning to reverse itself.

At the end of a historical review and current status report in any developing field, there is a temptation to applaud the advances in the field over the obsolete body of past knowledge and extoll the virtues of the present status. This exercise has its appeal, for it leaves the writer and reader alike feeling satisfied. However, much of the obsolete knowledge has survived, when it should have expired, and boasting is hardly in order. The conclusions that may be drawn at this point are related more to the concerns of psychologists about quality or impact. The challenge ahead is to develop systematic ways of bringing the very best of scientific and professional knowledge to bear on justice problems.

Functional Areas of Psychological Activity

2

David Twain, Richard McGee and
Lawrence A. Bennett

The agencies of government established to apply the criminal law are basically concerned with controlling socially undesirable human behavior. Ideas of deterrence, rehabilitation, retribution, and incapacitation are woven together into complex and often irrational patterns. These concepts reach back centuries before psychology was recognized as a legitimate scholarly discipline. The study and practice of psychology is a recent and, therefore, often suspect addition to the judgmental and decision-making processes arising from the application of criminal law.

The psychologist, then, is a relatively new actor in an ancient play. As his role develops, it must perforce affect the roles of the older, more established actors: the policeman, the judge, the jailer, and the correctional personnel, as well as the staffs in probation, parole, and community programs. In this accommodation of related roles, that played by the psychologist, no doubt, will change also.

The present chapter is concerned with existing and changing functions of the psychologist. It is directed at both the justice administrator who may utilize the services of a psychologist and, also, the psychologist who has had little exposure to justice agencies. Justice systems need all the professional and scientific help they can attract to help them make more rapid progress toward realizing their mandates. Among those that have worked within the Criminal Justice System (CJS), and who have not fulfilled their potential contributions, one can list the psychologist.

16   The roles and activities of psychology are broad and varied. One paramount function of the psychologist is that of the knowledge-builder. Another major role identifies him as a user of knowledge in the service of rational change. The locus of this change may be in the behavior of an individual, a small group, or an organization.

Psychologists work in programs and institutional settings similar to those of justice agencies, but many react unfavorably to the idea of working within the justice system. Indeed, there are some justice agency psychologists who believe that their ideas and best talents are underutilized. They feel constrained to routine and bureaucratic programs and, in some settings, to a steady diet of crisis. This reputed low status, low pay, and underutilization has kept many psychologists out of justice agencies and from functioning in the very program in which they want to play a developmental role.

These circumstances are detrimental to justice agencies and also to the field of psychology. There is much information to be learned about effective human service programs and organizational change that could be gathered in justice settings. On the other hand, many agencies suffer from both a lack of knowledge and from a lack of scientists and professionals who could help them to utilize the knowledge that is currently available.

In a number of justice agencies, psychologists have wide professional latitude, high status, competitive pay, and ready access to decision-makers. In these agencies, such as the Federal Bureau of Prisons and the Los Angeles Police Department, a joint learning process does, indeed, occur. Psychologists should be, and are, attracted to these kinds of criminal justice agencies.

ASSESSMENT SERVICES

Among the many functions alluded to in the previous section, the psychologist provides diagnostic services on a rather broad, general basis, for a variety of clients at several stages in the criminal justice system: pre-sentence, probation, correctional institution programming, and release to parole. This is probably one of the earliest applications of the skills of the psychologist to be used in the correctional system. It continues to receive the major emphasis in most programs.

The assessment targets range from the measurement of attitudes, or aptitudes, and personnel selection, to diagnosis of psychopathology. The skills required encompass construction, selection, utilization and interpretation of procedure for the objective assessment of individual potential or disability. More specific diagnostic skills are demanded when the need is related to the program management of specific problem individuals. Thus, assessment of organic brain damage, mental retardation, psychotic processes, and special educational or vocational needs may be required.

Unfortunately, in developing psychological services, undue emphasis is

often placed upon the diagnostic aspect, such as developing definitive descriptions of individuals and their psychological condition, far beyond the capabil-
ity of that system to provide any ameliorative services.

Offender rehabilitation programs, like those in other human service
fields, are just beginning to realize the potential impact of the differential
utilization of personnel, based on personal characteristics including interpersonal style. In selecting change agents, the question becomes: What man
with what characteristics is appropriate for what rehabilitative task? During
the past decade, for instance, the evidence has mounted that different "kinds"
of treatment personnel have differential impact in a behavior changing situation when matched with a varied client population. Maximum treatment
effectiveness results when the treater has been carefully matched with the
client. Some notable progress is being made with regard to this difficult
proposition, but further study needs to be undertaken for adequate performance of this task.

As criminal justice programs increasingly move toward a rehabilitative
stance, it will be a rare employee who will not double in brass. Aside from the
specialist specifically hired for a "treatment" role, most employees, through
example or informal association, have clearly demonstrated their impact on
client behavior. Each employee, be he policeman, court clerk, or correctional
guard, plays multiple roles in crime prevention and control. Each participant
in the preventive or rehabilitative process should be carefully screened and an
assessment made of his maximum potential contribution. Attention should be
directed toward selecting those with inherent talent as well as deterring employment of those unable to handle the interpersonal demands of this type
of work.

As programs change so will job descriptions. Psychologists with experience in areas relating to job description, job analysis, aptitude and attitude
measurement, and employee selection, have a major contribution to make in
maintaining, as well as building, an effective staff.

TREATMENT

In this area, the psychologist, along with the psychiatrist, psychiatric
social worker, and other individuals trained in the mental health field, provide
a wide variety of psychotherapeutic services at the various stages of the
criminal justice continuum.

The clinical psychologist group contains practitioners of every form of
non-medical psychotherapeutic intervention, from individual psychotherapy
to family therapy, and on to therapy with large groups, including collaboration with a variety of para-professional treatment personnel. From court
diversion projects to police intervention in crisis situations, and on to inmate
group psychotherapy in a correctional setting, the psychologist (as an expert

18 in psychopathology and behavior change technique) is typically a significant figure in treatment programs.

Many changes in program structure are being called for and innovation is taking place. Courts and legislatures are attempting to divest themselves of involvement in certain forms of victimless, sexual, and status offenses.[1] Correctional programs are moving toward community-based programming, thereby preserving or attempting to create pro-social ties to the community. In this process, the psychologist has profited a great deal from community mental health programs; this is knowledge that can be transplanted into justice settings. The psychologist also has a significant contribution to make with regard to "special" client-community problem areas that cut across many social agency jurisdictions. The drug addict, the alcoholic, the juvenile delinquent, and the mentally retarded or mentally-ill offender are manifestations of such "special" individual and social problem areas.

TRAINING

There continues to be a need for the broad training of personnel in almost all areas of the criminal justice system. An improved understanding of the psychological functioning of people, in general, and the criminal justice client, in particular, is needed. Almost all workers in the criminal justice system should have considerable training in managing individuals undergoing emotional distress. The psychologist's skills and training should also be utilized in training staff in the special attitudes and techniques required for unique programs. Inasmuch as a great deal of justice work involves "people relating to people," considerable effort needs to be directed toward assisting employees in gaining a greater awareness of how their personality dynamics may foster or inhibit their relationships with the clients.

Program innovations require the retraining of current personnel or the training of new employees for the new functions. This critical step is often forgotten; the omission is as responsible for program failure as any other contingency.

Psychologists are trainers. Approximately half of all psychologists earn their living through the educational enterprise (more, if one stretches the definition of teacher). The psychologist, in collaboration with other educational personnel, can effectively assume a number of educational, training, and counseling roles which are currently either poorly represented or are non-existent in justice agencies.

The burgeoning field of the para-professional is representative of the attempt to meet the need for trained justice personnel. Psychologists were

---

[1]Status offenders are usually juveniles committed to state institutions for behavior (e.g., incorrigible) which would not be an offense if performed by adults.

among the pioneers in the development of para-professionals; and justice agencies provided a setting for some of the earliest experimental training programs.

Psychological skills in the area of education and training should, of course, be directed to the CJS client. Preparation for work and job placement are as good a bet for crime prevention as any other; they have not been given their due. The psychologist skilled in education and the expert in vocational training and placement could be joined by the industrially trained psychologist for program development in this area. It is suggested that the use by clinical or counseling psychologists of other psychological expertise, may increase the range of available skills and contributions.

CONSULTATION

Contributors from all of the behavioral sciences are often called upon to work with administrators in a variety of planning activities. This may range from the design of a specific treatment project to an analysis of the impact of a contemplated program change in an ongoing system. Another area where such knowledge and skills can be well utilized is in the coordinated utilization of mental health resources outside the traditional confines of criminal justice. For example, many community mental health services can make a contribution to the county jail system and act in an advisory capacity to the courts.

Some clinically trained psychologists feel that it is poor strategy, and a great waste of time and money, to employ fully trained psychologists to provide direct service functions for justice systems. They believe that through consultation, the psychologist can best utilize his knowledge by extending his skills to others. This training has successfully worked with the police in enhancing their capacity for dealing with problems, ranging from the handling of suicide attempts to the management of panicky adolescents. Judges have been trained in interpersonal relations. Correctional officers have been trained to function as effective counselors and therapists. In this view, behavioral knowledge can be best infused into the justice system, when the psychologist is utilized as a consultant.

While clinical psychologists have traditionally been the specialists recruited to work in the correctional setting, the contributions of social psychologists are beginning to be recognized. For example, knowledge about psychological space may result in better facility planning. An understanding of the nature and operation of an organization may well lead to modification of lines of communication, a contribution that can be of considerable significance to the clients.

The involvement of behavioral scientists in business and industry is an additional analogue of the psychologist as consultant in program development and organizational change. Management has become increasingly aware that organizational structure, decision-making process, and other aspects of the system, influence program effectiveness.

The human services area has been slow to recognize the value of such services. A major reason for this condition is that human services agencies, while sporadically subject to severe public scrutiny, are relatively free from being held accountable for goal attainment or program impact. What is usually demanded is a minimal reporting of rather superficial statistics, the maintenance of a "clean" ship, and the accomplishment of unspecified "good" services.

In the recent past, human service organizations have begun to incorporate planning functions. However, these have been instituted only at the very highest organizational levels. In addition, the specialty of Community Psychology is developing and can be viewed as an early sign of increased demand in the human services for the skills of consultation and organizational-change technology.

It is at the level of "line" practitioners that psychological consultation should increasingly be employed. Many treatment activities can be entrusted to the well-trained para-professional, provided there is ample supervision by professionals. The psychologist as consultant and practitioner of vocational, clinical, and other rehabilitative or service programs, has two major mandates. On the one hand, he must strive to integrate his skills and functions to meet the realistic demands of the system, while remaining alert to the long range implications of his efforts. If this approach is appropriate and has positive impact, it will be communicated to all parts of the system. On the other hand, and clearly corollary to the above, the professional practitioner, whenever and wherever it is appropriate, must attempt to "give his skills away." He can and should extend his competence through well-trained para-professional personnel who, it has been found, bring many other useful traits and attitudes into the program arena. Through this type of activity, the role and function of the full professional will be clarified and his impact maximized.

RESEARCH AND THEORY BUILDING

The training of the psychologist as a scientist qualifies him to contribute knowledge through research. This may range from the study of the impact of psychotherapy to the development of special predictive tools for determining readiness for parole. He can direct the efforts of a correctional system along theoretical lines which allow for the systematic accumulation of purposeful knowledge. Thus, he can help build a knowledge base of descriptive data, design effective program monitoring activities, and devise means for the evaluation of programs. The impact of the psychologist's contributions can be fully realized through response to feedback information which relates to goal-setting behavior.

In addition to supplying theoretical knowledge (i.e., basic research), 21
the psychologist who designs and implements program evaluative studies can
have a profound impact on a justice system. The California Probation
Subsidy Program and The Kennedy Youth Center of Morgantown, West
Virginia, are but two examples of this process in action. The following chapters
address this topic in detail.

ORGANIZATION OF PSYCHOLOGICAL SERVICES

It is beyond the scope of this discussion to identify and develop
patterns for effective utilization of psychological services. There are many
unique organizational structures within which psychologists might beneficially be employed. However, four pertinent observations can be made. The
first three are based on the assumption that eventually there will be sufficient
psychologists available to meet the needs of selected agencies.

First, it has been clearly observed that most mental health professionals
have a "flocking" tendency. If you have three psychologists and a vacancy,
you can probably recruit the fourth one. If you have an agency with one
vacancy, it may never be filled. Thus, whenever possible, psychological
services should be organized in such a way that psychologists, other behavioral
scientists, and mental health professionals in adjacent jurisdictions can be
grouped together both physically, and in terms of supervision, to take advantage of this natural tendency. Interest, motivation, professional produc-
tivity, and creativity can be achieved by maintaining a high level of interdisciplinary, as well as intradisciplinary, stimulation.

Second, psychologists, like many other professional groups, experience
a chronic state of identity crisis. Thus, rather than being routinely promoted
into administrative positions, the individual psychologist may be more effective if he is identified as such and delegated additional responsibilities in
consultation with top level administration. His professionalism should be
fostered by encouraging attendance at professional meetings.

Third, there has to be direct access to top management. Psychologists,
like every other minority group in modern day society, want a piece of the
action. If they are buried beneath a multi-layered bureaucracy, they feel the
knowledge they can contribute to the system is squelched, buried, or distorted.
If psychologists can be grouped together, then the supervisor of such a unit
can be designated as a member of high-level executive committees; this
assures every psychologist in the system that his views and ideas can be fully
considered by top administration.

Fourth, many psychologists should take key positions and often function as consultants. This is based on the assumption that there now are, and
will continue to be, few psychologists available to the system. Thus, in order
to maximize their impact and contribution, these provisions need to be made.

22   THE DEVELOPMENT OF PRIORITIES

We have outlined demands and duties that would require a quantity of psychologists far in excess of those currently employed in criminal justice systems, and probably exceeding the number that might be available, given limited manpower resources. Therefore, some determination has to be made as to which among the many potential contributions will be the most important in moving the system forward.

If we accept the fact that it is unlikely that mental health professionals will be available in sufficient numbers to meet the mental health needs of society as a whole, then we must decide how some priorities can be met in a different fashion. This demand/need ratio is even more pronounced in the justice system. It suggests that many of the direct impact programs will have to be manned by non-professional personnel. This, as we noted, means that the talents of the few existing psychologists must be multiplied by transmitting skills to others through intensive programs of training and consultation.

Further, if the criminal justice system (particularly corrections) is to advance, new ideas and approaches must be entertained. Here again, the psychologist can play a key role as consultant to administrators in the systematic planning of new programs, in the development of techniques for evaluating alternatives, and in the study of the effectiveness of various aspects of the system. Further, in the absence of an administrative structure that permits these roles, he should act to establish them through an Office of Program Planning and Evaluation, or a similar organizational mechanism.

Priority #1:
Definition of Problem and Goal Setting[2]

Every organization is given a mandate and has constraints imposed upon it by superordinate and counterpart structures in the larger system. Each organization should endeavor to participate as fully as possible in shaping its unique function. The process of program development calls for a clear definition of the problem to be addressed by the intervening organization: determination of important needs, values, constraints, and the careful establishment of goals, both long and short range. This aspect of program planning is critical to program development, but in the human services area it is usually given insufficient attention and resources. Since programs change continuously, the planning process and program development are ongoing functions. The area of planning as defined here should be given high priority for the employment of appropriately skilled psychologists.

---

[2]The priorities listed here are those prepared by David Twain for the Lake Wales Conference on Psychology and Justice.

Priority #2:

The Need for Information

The planning process is dependent on information. Typically, such information is not readily available. There is a major movement currently underway in the criminal justice system to develop a descriptive data base for administrative decision-making at all levels, throughout the system. Research positions are being established in the administrative offices of the courts. Computerized management information systems are being established in police headquarters and in probation offices.

Once the planning function has been established, the highest priority for the use of psychology is the development of necessary information. Initially, the task will be to "map the system," that is, to build a descriptive data base. Collection and analysis of data will be addressed to the nature of the problems targeted by the organization: client characteristics, personnel characteristics, and so on.

As old programs are sharpened and new programs evolve, they will be further enhanced by monitoring informational activities that help determine whether the program is functioning as it was designed. Does the program have discernable impact and in what ways?

The informational activities described and the associated activity of action-research call on skills possessed by psychologists but probably not by any single psychologist. A brief list of such skills includes operations analysis, management-information-systems design, research design, test construction, and statistical application. A host of related skills range from proposal writing to the capacity for working with administrators and practitioners in building a research strategy that maximizes program potential.

Priority #3:

Direct Services to the Client

This chapter has identified a panoply of education, training and treatment services that are functions of psychology. The quality and utilization of these "line" services are the critical element in program payoff. Most of these services are useful and necessary in helping offenders learn to help themselves. The great problem has been and continues to be the ineffective and inappropriate use of these services throughout the system.

The rationale for ordering the priorities presented here is to create a structure for enhancing the utility of such services and for determining which services are most useful in what problem areas. The hope is to move away from fads, hunches and crises, and toward more rational decision-making.

SUMMARY

This chapter has attempted to outline the major roles and functions of

24   psychologists in the justice system. Not only does it emphasize the need for an expanded scope of activities in order that professional psychologists can make optimal use of their skills, but it also realistically subscribes to the need to implement programs employing para-professionals. Since demands far exceed the resources to meet them, a set of priorities has been proposed. While the specifics contained in these paragraphs can be challenged, the overriding conclusion cannot be avoided: careful planning and forethought are required if the justice system is to fully realize and profit from the talents of its psychological personnel.

Five Challenges

Don M. Gottfredson

Psychologists are uniquely qualified to contribute solutions to five of the most pressing and difficult problems confronting the field of corrections and related social agencies. These problems are pressing not only because so many lives are so severely disrupted by criminal behavior and by the societal responses to that behavior but also in view of an increasing national disenchantment with the effectiveness of any prevention or correctional programs. These problems are difficult not only because they are complex but also because their solutions will require manpower and hard work. Psychologists are well-equipped to tackle these problems by dint not only of their scientific tradition but also by reason of their concern for individual persons and the alleviation of misery.

The history of criminal justice shows that in the treatment of persons convicted of crimes we have been at worst inhumane, at best inefficient, and at all times confused. Psychologists can lessen the confusion, increase efficiency, and contribute to providing a more humane criminal justice system; they can do these things by meeting the five challenges to be described.

The first challenge is to lessen the confusion by developing an internally consistent theoretical framework. This will undoubtedly require acceptance of the second challenge: that of defining person classifications with demonstrable relevance to specified goals. This challenge is related to the third, which is to develop and test effective treatment and control programs.

26   The fourth challenge is to monitor the ability of agencies to achieve their goals; and the fifth is to develop and test ways to ensure that the results of these efforts are communicated and used.

THE NEED FOR INTEGRATION OF THEORIES

Nothing is so practical as a good theory, according to an often-quoted comment by Kurt Lewin. A good theory guides both practice and research; in addition, it helps to bring about their integration by providing a basis for action research yielding new knowledge.

In building theories, much attention has been given to delinquency, little to adult crime, and almost none to corrections. As noted by Klein (1967), texts on corrections "are as likely as not to omit the very word, theory, from their indexes"; Conrad's *Crime and Its Correction* (1965) employs the word theory only to note its lack in corrections; and Empey (Klein, 1967) describes correctional policies and activities as "guided by a kind of intuitive, goal-oriented guessing . . . ." Empirical tests of theories, and of effectiveness of action programs, have been woefully inadequate or have not been attempted.

If rigorous criteria of a "good" theory were listed, it could be shown readily that existing theories of delinquency and crime do not hold up well under examination. There is no available comprehensive, internally consistent theoretical framework to impose order and guide research and practice in corrections. We are not wholly ignorant of the precursors to anti-social conduct or of requirements for its modification; but the needed comprehensive system, building upon presently available knowledge and earlier theory, has not yet been developed.

A selective, noncomprehensive review of contributions to theory requires their arbitrary classification. While any classification probably will not be to the liking of the theorists, it will serve at least to depict the diversity of approaches which have been taken. Besides the earliest theories—including those of Bentham and Beccaria, whose writings continue to exert a profound influence on contemporary views of crime, the law, and punishment—most approaches fall within five general groups: (a) psychogenic, (b) social, (c) physiological, (d) constitutional, and (e) economic.

The psychogenic theories, emphasizing the personality or psychological functioning of the individual in the development of delinquent or criminal behavior, may be classified (in terms of their historical development or central concerns) as analytic, phenomenological, or behavioral. The classification is unsatisfactory because of overlapping concerns, but it serves to point up the magnitude of the problem of integration of the widely divergent theoretical viewpoints which guide psychological research and practice in corrections.

The basic concepts of analytic theories have proven difficult to oper-

ationalize, with the consequence that experimental verification or refutation
is exceedingly difficult. Yet, the central arguments that delinquent and
criminal behavior results from a failure of effective ego or superego controls
due to faulty early training or parental neglect (Alexander & Staub, 1956) or,
alternatively, that it represents a symptomatic method of coping with a basic
problem of adjustment—that is, defense against anxiety (Healy & Bronner,
1936; Aichorn, 1935; Alexander & Healy, 1935)—guide much clinical
practice. The promise of the resulting model for corrections, based upon
speculations concerning the origins and proper treatment of the mentally ill,
has not been matched by achievement; and research workers seem either to
have decided that science is not up to testing the theory (and returned to
clinical practice) or that the theory is not up to science (and turned to
alternative theories). Analytic theories overlap with phenomenological approaches in asserting that the determinants of behavior are often not reality
features of the person's environment but the individual's perception of that
reality. The overlap with behavioral theories is an emphasis upon the importance of learning.

Phenomenological theories focus upon the postulates that behavior,
including acts defined as delinquent, is a product of the individual's perceptions. They may be illustrated by approaches stressing the development of
interpersonal maturity or of cognition.

Sullivan, Grant, and Grant (1956) extensively developed a concept of
personality maturity levels for a classification of persons thought to have
relevance for treatment of those who become defined as "delinquent" or as
adult "offenders." Successive levels of "integration" are defined by the
diagnosed perceptual abilities of the person and produce characteristic modes
of interpersonal relations. Reports of treatment research at a naval retraining
command and also in a community treatment program for "delinquents"—
the latter based upon further extension of the theory by Warren (Grant &
Grant, 1959; Warren, 1969)—support the view, explicit in the theory, that
different types of "offenders" require different types of treatment.

Cognitive theories tend to stress the person's interpretation and cognitive
response to the environment, with variations in such response leading to a
perceived legitimacy of deviant behavior. Examples of important conceptions
of such approaches include "self-definitions" which insulate against delinquency (Reckless, Dinitz, & Kay, 1967; Reckless, Dinitz, & Murray, 1956;
Scarpitti, Murray, Dinitz, & Reckless, 1962); of "techniques of neutralization" which provide rationalizations decreasing behavioral restraints (Sykes &
Matza, 1967); or of "stigmatization" (the labeling of persons as "bad,"
"delinquent," or "criminal") reinforcing self-perceptions and creating a "self-
fulfilling prophesy" (Lemert, 1951; Lentz, 1966; Nat. Counc. on Crime
Delinquency, 1964; Schwartz & Skolnick, 1964; Tannenbaum, 1938).

The concept central to behavioral theories is learning; and learning

28   principles developed initially in psychological laboratories now have led to an impressive body of knowledge concerning the acquisition, control, and modification of behavior. The resulting technology has been applied to a variety of clinical problems; a 1966 summary emphasizing application to delinquent and criminal behavior prepared by Shah (1966) reviews the most relevant theoretical work, techniques of behavior modification, and implications of this approach, which emphasizes the utilization of learning theory, the experimental analysis of behavior, and the development of explicit, observable, and precise procedures. Behavioral approaches seek to establish lawful relationship between operationally defined sets of behaviors and environmental variables; thus, for example, concepts such as "reinforcement," "punishment," or "extinction" do not constitute postulates or hypotheses—rather, they are constructs defined by such functional relationships and constitute descriptions of observed relationships.

Behavior modification approaches mainly are based upon the operant conditioning principles specified by Skinner (1953), although some are derived directly from the classical conditioning model (Salter, 1961) and some have drawn guiding principles from Hull (Eysenck, 1960), Guthrie (Patterson, 1965), and others. The classical conditioning theory approach is exemplified by Wolpe (1958): autonomic nervous system responses, the physiological concomitant of anxiety, may be arranged to occur at very low, manageable levels; the general technique for avoiding anxiety in a specific situation is to condition a response incompatible with anxiety—commonly relaxation—thus making possible a desensitization process. Techniques based upon operant conditioning principles, in contrast, usually attempt to deal directly with maladaptive behavior rather than any underlying events.

Work in this area in recent years has tended to move from the laboratory to work in institutional settings and hence to work in natural environments; and this progress has important implications for the corrections field, which increasingly is giving emphasis to community-based treatment approaches in preference to institutional programs. Notable examples of serious attempts to develop and test large-scale programs in correctional institutions are those of Cohen (1965) in the National Training School for Boys, of McKee (1964) at the Draper Correctional Institution in Alabama, and of Jesness (1972) in the California Youth Authority. Attempts to modify behavior in the natural environment are exemplified by the studies of Tharp and Wetzel (1969) and by the clinical reports which they cite. Similarly, Schwitzgebel (1964) found his young delinquent subjects in pool halls and on street corners, as did Slack (1960); and Thorne, Tharp, and Wetzel (1967) discussed implications of behavior modification for probation work.

Despite the overlapping concerns, the basic premises of analytic, phenomenological, and behavioral theories are widely divergent; and the

theoretical integration called for will be a difficult task even within the 29
psychogenic approaches. What about the other theoretical frames of reference?

Social theories with implications for corrections have been influenced
especially by Durkheim (1956) and Merton (1957), the latter's theory
focusing on the ambivalence toward norms which arises when common goals
are proclaimed for all, while social structure restricts access to the approved
means of reaching these goals for certain segments of it—with the dis-
enfranchised resorting to deviant means of attainment. Notable contemporary social-psychological theories include the conceptions of differential
association as advanced by Sutherland (1955) and modified by Cressey
(1962), both of whom emphasize the learning that takes place in intimate
personal groups; and various workers have attempted to increase the veri-
fiability of the theory (Glaser, 1960), recast its conceptions into operant
learning theory (Burgess & Akers, 1966), or empirically test hypotheses
derived from it (Short, 1958; Voss, 1964; Erickson & Empey, 1965). A
particularly noteworthy example is provided also by the opportunity structure
theory of Cloward and Ohlin (1961), which emphasizes the nature of the
community's integration of legitimate and illegitimate means with cultural
goals as determining the nature of delinquent accomodations to goal
achievement and which has been widely influential in planning delinquency
programs and later "war on poverty" programs. These social theories have
provided a prolific source of suggestions for practical steps which can be
taken to reduce delinquency and crime; but the many opportunities to test
the programs developed from these conceptions unfortunately have not been
taken.

Physiological anomalies or dysfunctions have been hypothesized by
many writers to be among the precursors to delinquent and criminal behavior,
and the possible importance in individual cases particularly of brain damage,
endocrine dysfunction, or nutritional deficiencies is well known to clinicians.
Since 1965, considerable attention has been given to a rare genetic abnormal-
ity—the XYY constitution—which seems to be associated with persistent
aggressive behavior; a number of research workers are actively studying this
topic.[3]

The constitutional theories, most notably of Kretschmer (1925) and
Sheldon (1940, 1942), which emphasize the role of physique and associated
temperament in the development of delinquency are well known to psychologists, but the results of empirical efforts on this topic rarely are incorporated
in theory building.

---

[3] A number of these studies are funded by the National Institute of Mental
Health's Crime and Delinquency Center, including Witkin's R01-17653, "The XYY Syn-
drome," Waxman's R03-17171, "XYY Individuals Among Hawaiian Delinquent Population," and Borgaonkar's P01-17565, "Genetics of the XYY Phenomena in Man."

30   Delinquency and crime have been linked to economic conditions by a number of writers (Bonger, 1967) and by the President's Commission on Law Enforcement and Administration of Justice (1967).

Confronted with this diversity of theoretical conceptions of delinquent and criminal behavior, one may ask what kinds of theories are needed or are apt to be most useful. Do we need theories of delinquency—or do we need theories of the development of delinquency behavior, of the process by which behavior becomes defined as delinquent, of the processes by which delinquency behavior may be prevented or controlled, of the processes of effective treatment of adjudicated delinquents, of effective management systems or of "rehabilitation" or behavior modification? Do we need all of these, or do we need some for some purposes, some for others? Is presently available information, and the "state of the art" so insufficiently developed as to suggest that any attempts toward a single, unified theory are destined to be futile? Is it sufficient, for present purposes, to specify single hypotheses to justify isolated research efforts.

The words "delinquent" and "criminal" are popular in common usage in technical literature; but are they useful concepts? These labels are used frequently as if they described a state of the person; but clearly they do not (Wilkins & Gottfredson, 1969). The common analogy between crime and illness breaks down immediately when it is realized that "crimes" relate to a combination of person(s) and event(s). Although one may operationally define a "criminal" as a person who has committed a crime (any crime, if we do not care that the definition now includes the whole population!) or as a persons convicted of a crime, or incarcerated for a crime, or the like, such descriptions are not descriptions of the state of the *person*; rather, they are descriptions of the state or stage of the *system* with which the person is involved because of his or her acts. The number of persons awaiting trial provides no description of the persons involved; it provides rather an opportunity for assessment of the delays of the criminal justice system.

Perhaps it will be argued that the label "criminal" does indeed describe a "state of the person," and we know what we mean by calling someone that name—apart from reference to any specific behavioral acts or external events. If so, can we specify *when* a person becomes a "criminal"? Do we accept the belief that "once a criminal always a criminal" and, if not, can we tell when a criminal is no longer a criminal? How, by examination of him, physically, medically, psychologically, or any other way can we say when he has moved out of the state of "being criminal"?

If conviction for a crime does not define a state of the person, then it does not define a need for treatment, since it is not possible to treat an event but only a state. There may be social, medical, psychological, or other "states" which may be ascribed to individuals; and these states may tend to increase the probability of crime. We may seek to "treat," i.e., modify these states; but this requires their careful and explicit definition.

Psychologists of a behavioristic inclination will find this whole diversion as unnecessary as the concept "state of the person" itself. If states of the person must be defined in terms of stimulus conditions (events) and responses (acts) anyhow, what is the need for the concept? Perhaps one answer is to be found in the heuristic value of the person-classification approaches discussed below, which have more often stemmed from psychogenic or phenomenological frames of reference.

This cursory review of some of the leading approaches to explanations of delinquency and crime is intended only to suggest the diversity of theories that have been advanced. The literature on each of the approaches mentioned is vast; and, similarly, there is an extensive literature on psychological differences between delinquent and nondelinquent populations and on the related topic of prediction, much of which has implications for theory. Thus, the problem is posed: how can a variety of overlapping, yet conflicting psychological theories be merged with the most useful features of the social theories, psychological evidence, and other approaches into an integrated theoretical framework? Further, how can this framework be combined with more explicit statements of the objectives and methods of correctional agencies? The lack of a comprehensive, internally consistent, verifiable theory of delinquency to guide action programs to increased effectiveness poses a major challenge to our field.

Whether or not this is the most critical challenge, however, is open to question. William James had, in 1888, something to say about the role of the psychologist. In a letter to Hugo Munsterberg, he said,

> Whose theories in Psychology have any definitive value today? No ones! Their only use is to sharpen further reflection and observation. The man who throws out the most new ideas and immediately seeks to subject them to experimental control is the most useful Psychologist in the present state of the science [Knight, 1954].

His comment still is relevant, and in corrections the new ideas and testing needed have to do with offender classification, with program evaluation of agency effectiveness, and with research utilization.

THE NEED FOR IMPROVED CLASSIFICATION METHODS

A variety of studies recently has shown the need for improved schemes for classification of persons in view of evidence supporting a differential effectiveness of treatment programs upon various subsets of populations (Argyle, 1961; Grant, M. Q., 1961; Grant & Grant, 1959; Warren, 1969; Adams, 1961).

A recent review (Grant, M. Q., 1961) suggests there have been five general approaches to this classification problem.

There have been psychiatrically-oriented approaches, represented, for example, by the work of Jenkins and Hewitt (1944), Redl (1956), Erikson

32 (1950), Aichorn (1935), Bloch and Flynn (1956), Argyle (1961), the Illinois State Training School for Boys Treatment Committee (1935), the California Youth Authority Standard Nomenclature Committee (1958), and Cormier (1959).

There have been classification studies related to the social theories mentioned previously, for example, in the reference group typologies proposed by Schragg (1944) and Sykes (1958) and in social class typologies as exemplified by Miller (1959).

There have been behavior classifications related to either offense types or conformity-nonconformity, such as those of Gibbons and Garrity (1958), Ohlin (1951), Reckless (1950), and Lejins (1954).

There have been classification schemes which rest upon assumptions regarding social perception or interpersonal interaction such as those of Gough and Peterson (1952); Peterson, Quay, and Cameron (1959); and Sullivan, Grant, and Grant (1956); and there has been at least one instrument based upon cognition, measuring information possessed concerning significant others (Venezia, 1968).

Finally, there have been a number of empirically derived classification procedures, mainly developed in relation to prediction methods. These include the Mannheim and Wilkins (1955) Borstall studies in Great Britain; base expectancy studies by Gottfredson and Beverly (1962) and others; configuration analysis procedures as used by Glaser (1962) and by Babst (1968); association analysis procedures as employed by Gottfredson and Ballard (1963); and cluster analysis methods, as used by Fildes and Gottfredson (1971).

An excellent recent discussion by Warren (1971) shows there is a considerable communality among many of these and other classification systems. Table 3 is adapted from a chart in her paper, which includes an outstanding set of references on this topic, including those to the typologies listed in the table. (It should be mentioned here, as by Warren, that the cross-classifications shown were not checked with the authors, and that one—namely Quay (1964)—views his system not as a typology but as having reference to dimensions of behavior.)

The table suggests that six classification bands can be identified tentatively as cutting across various typologies; these Warren entitled Asocial, Conformist, Antisocial-manipulation, Neurotic, Subcultural-Identifier and Situational Offender. The consistencies in the data from the typological studies reviewed, and the communalities across differing theoretical viewpoints, provide encouraging signs toward an eventual integration.

Warren (1971) also found signs of an increasing integration of psychological and sociological viewpoints in the area of classification. Citing examples, such as Cloward and Ohlin and Cohen, and her own integration attempts, she stated:

Sociologists continue to accuse psychological typologists of taking insufficient 33 cognizance of environmental factors; psychologists continue to accuse sociological typologists of having insufficient regard for intra-psychic factors. Nevertheless, it is now possible to find investigators who are attempting to theoretically link the sociological, psychological, and situational variables which are all relevant to a completely satisfactory taxonomy [Warren, 1971].

All these classification schemes, which are illustrative and not exhaustive, are not equally valuable for all purposes—some have more direct treatment implications than others; some are demonstrably more reliable than others; some are more helpful in generating testable hypotheses than others; and in only a few instances has the relevance of the classification for treatment placement been clearly demonstrated. Thus, the need is great for development of theoretically sound, clinically useful, testable classification systems, with enunciation of the probable etiology, proposed treatment or control measures, and for demonstration of the effectiveness of differential treatment placements.

The importance of person classifications at each step in the "correctional continuum" from conviction to discharge should be emphasized. To the extent that criminal justice agencies adopt goals of modifying behavior to reduce the probability of law violations, it is important to have available at each decision point (concerning placement decisions) classification information which will indicate the setting and methods most likely to achieve those goals. In the absence of any classification system, no interactions of person x treatment on outcome measures can be observed; and there is now considerable evidence that such interactions are critically important.

THE NEED FOR SYSTEMATIC PROGRAM EVALUATION

The development of improved offender classification methods should be included with the development and testing of the improved treatment programs that constitute the third major challenge to correctional psychologists. Within correctional agencies, little emphasis has been given to the general problem of evaluating effectiveness of programs. The 1967 report of the President's Crime Commission pointed out that the nation spends more than $4 billion annually on the criminal justice system, but

the expenditure for the kinds of descriptive, operational, and evaluative research that are obvious prerequisites for a rational system of crime control is negligible. Almost every industry makes a significant investment in research each year. Approximately 15 percent of the Defense Department's annual budget is allocated to research.

The Commission (1967) noted that only a small fraction of 1% of the total expenditures for crime control is spent on research and added, "There is probably no subject of comparable concern to which the Nation is devoting so many resources and so much effort with so little knowledge of

TABLE 3

Cross-Classification of Offender Typologies

Subtypes	Jesness	Hunt	Hurwitz	Mac-Gregor	Makkay	Quay	Reiss	Warren
1/Asocial		Sub I	Type II	Schizophrenic	Antisocial Character Disorder-Primitive	Unsocialized-psychopath		I_2
Aggressive	Immature, aggressive				Aggressive			Asocial, aggressive
Passive	Immature, passive				Passive-aggressive			Asocial, passive
2/Conformist		Stage I			Antisocial Character Disorder-Organized			·I_3
Nondelinquently-oriented	Immature, passive				Passive-aggressive	Inadequate-immature		Conformist Immature
Delinquently-oriented	Socialized conformist					/?Subcultural/	/?Relatively integrated/	Conformist Cultural
3/Antisocial-manipulator	Manipulator			Autocrat	Antisocial Character Disorder-Organized Aggressive		Defective superego	I_3 Manipulator
4/Neurotic		Stage II	Type II		Neurotic		Relatively weak ego	I_4 Neurotic
Acting-out	Neurotic-acting out							Neurotic, acting-out
Anxious	Neurotic, anxious			Intimidated				
	Neurotic, depressed					Neurotic-disturbed		Neurotic, anxious
5/Subcultural-identifier	Cultural delinquent	Stage II	Type II	Rebel	Subcultural	Subcultural	Relatively Integrated	I_4 Cultural Identifier
6/Situational		Stage II						I_4 Situational, emotional reaction
Types not cross-classified					Mental Retardate Psychotic			

APA	Argyle	Gibbons	Jenkins & Hewitt	McCord	Reckless	Schrag	Studt
Passive-aggressive personality	Lack of sympathy					Asocial	Isolate
Aggressive		Overly aggressive	Unsocialized aggressive				
Passive-aggressive							
Passive-aggressive personality	Inadequate superego			Conformist			
							Receiver
Passive-dependent		Gang offenders	/?Socialized/			Antisocial	
Antisocial personality	Inadequate superego			Aggressive (psychopathic)	Psychopath	Pseudosocial	Manipulator
Sociopathic personality disturbance	Weak ego control				Neurotic Personality	Prosocial	
		Joyrider					Loveseeker
		Behavior problems	Overinhibited	Neurotic-withdrawn			
Dyssocial reaction	Deviant identification	Gang offenders	Socialized			Antisocial	Learner
Adjustment reaction of adolescence		Casual delinquent		Offenders of the moment			
		Heroin user female delinquent		Eruptive behavior			

36 what it is doing." Unfortunately, the observation still seems up-to-date.
What is needed, in every correctional agency, is a system providing for
continuous program evaluation as an aid to the administration, management,
and program development of the organization. There are four basic features
to this framework; they are inter-related and interdependent, as the word
system implies.

The *first* feature is available to us: it is a laboratory for social
research and action. We have failed to realize the potential contribution to
science and to the alleviation of misery of the laboratories provided by the
nature of correctional agencies. The *second* feature is a system for collection
and storage of three kinds of information: in order to evaluate programs, we
need to collect information concerning the persons defined as offenders,
including the already suggested development of improved classification procedures, information describing the person's treatment exposure, and information describing outcomes in terms of goals of the agency. The *third* feature is
the collaborative use of what Cronbach (1957) termed the "two disciplines of
scientific psychology," namely correlational studies and experimental studies;
this can enable us to invest the scarce resources of research time where the
likelihood of increased knowledge is greater. *Fourth*, provisions for furnishing
information to agency decision-makers are required, and upon the effective
communication to research results hinges their utilization in practice.

If such a framework is to be useful in program evaluation, explicit
descriptions of the programs being evaluated are needed as well. Without them,
attempts to evaluate programs may finish with a double disappointment: an
inability not only to state the program's accomplishment, but an inability
even to describe the program.

Correctional programs are usually changed on the basis of experience
gained as the program is developed. Program quality control procedures,
therefore, are needed in order to ensure that programs are run in accord with
a plan or that the plan—and not only the program—is modified. This need has
been well-stated by Pearl (1962):

> the basic concern in an experiment (to investigate the effectiveness of a treatment
> program in a social agency) is the quality of the intervention and secondarily the
> quality of the measurement.
>
> Programs, no matter how well-designed or sound in theory are only as good as that
> which is put into practice. It is the highest of self-deception to inaugurate a pro-
> gram of high-sounding phrases while actually continuing to do business at the
> same old stand, in the same old way, with the same old procedures. The reverse of
> this could also be true. It is possible to institute effective innovations in . . . pro-
> grams without being aware of the nature of their impact.

Without careful record-keeping and documentation of changes in a
program plan, we never can assess the impact of the program adequately to
provide guidance for future program planning. Regardless of the program

outcomes—whether favorable or unfavorable in terms of agency goals—and even with careful follow-up study of these outcomes, the program cannot be described completely enough that others can repeat it. If the program was clearly described in advance, but changed as it was put into practice, and if the changes were not clearly spelled out, then the evaluation effort can only be misleading, resulting in the conclusion that the program is effective, or that it is ineffective, when that particular program never has been tried.

As part of the program description, the characteristics of the treaters often are overlooked. In a few studies, notably those of Gough (1956), of Glaser (1964), of Havel (1965), of the Grants (1959), and of Warren (1969), this problem has been given some attention. In the latter study, a major focus of the research is on the appropriate matching of the youth under supervision and the staff assigned treatment responsibility.

Similarly, measures of the treatment environment have been lacking, although they could contribute significantly to the evaluation of institutional programs. Conceptions of therapeutic communities, as exemplified by Maxwell Jones (1953), have markedly influenced correctional program development in a number of settings; but in the absence of methods for measurement of the perceptions of the environment by residents and staff, the precise nature of the impact of such changes cannot be determined. The studies of Moos (1968) and of Wenk (unpublished) provide examples of needed research in this area.

The utilization of persons, typically regarded as "subjects" in research or "recipients" of treatment, as *participants* in agency self-study efforts and programs aimed at both personal and social change, represents a significant departure from traditional, stereotyped thinking about who should do what, with what, and to whom in corrections. This movement, best exemplified by the work of Grant (1967) and of Toch (1969, 1970) also deserves careful descriptive work permitting its assessment.

The collaborative use of experimental and correlational methods for program evaluations provides, within any correctional agency, a basis for continual improvement of effectiveness. The two approaches, in combination, also can provide the analytic methods necessary to utilization of an information system to guide decision-makers at all levels in more rational program planning, treatment allocation, and control (Wilkins, 1961; Gottfredson, 1961).

A first requirement, however, often neglected in correctional research, is the explicit definition of program objectives. Correctional agencies, like persons, are apt to have not a single goal but many; like persons, they are apt to have some conflicting ones.

Much further work needs to be done to improve measures of program outcomes. A single example may illustrate the complexity of this problem— namely, the use of a parole violation criterion as a measure of favorable or unfavorable program outcome. Assume that parole violation is defined as any return to prison, or absconding from parole, or sentence to jail more than 60 days during a specified time period. Similar definitions have been used in many studies, and it is not argued here that this has not been useful as a crude measure of outcome. Yet, its serious limitations as an adequate outcome criterion are obvious. Setting aside the basic problem of reliability, what do we lack in this criterion? Of course, some of the guilty may not be caught, and some of the innocent may be wrongly classified as violators. A perhaps more serious problem is that, in addition, we have in every instance a classification based not only upon the behavior of the person under parole supervision but also upon the behavior of others—i.e., upon an administrative or judicial response to that behavior; and these two sources are "artificially tied [Brunswick, 1948]" in any analysis. Further, the dichotomous classification makes no allowance for the severity of the violation—nor does it include any notion of variation in the quality of adjustment achieved by those not classed as violators. Thus, no before and after comparisons of the severity of antisocial behavior are possible, and even the identification of monetary and social costs involved are extremely elusive. It is very apparent that improved measures of behavior to be classed as offensive deserve a high priority for research efforts.

Similar problems are posed throughout the delinquency and crime field, especially since we have at present no adequate measures of either delinquency or crime. The limitations of the Federal Bureau of Investigation's crime report series as measures of crime are well known (Doleschal, 1968); a number of studies have been of useful contributions through self-report studies (Gold); and the National Institute of Law Enforcement and Criminal Justice has initiated a large-scale victimization survey; each of these approaches contributes uniquely to the problem's solution, but each has limitations as a completely valid measure.

Once program objectives have been identified and explictly defined, the most rigorous approach to program evaluation remains the classic experimental design; but this approach alone, despite its power, is inadequate to the task of evaluating the variety of programs, often ardently advocated, but usually untested, which are in use in corrections. Some of the problems with classical experimental designs may be mentioned: experimental designs may be precluded by the nature of the problem, by law, or by ethical considerations; selective biases may creep in despite random allocation to comparison groups; control groups exposed to "no treatment" are impossible, since these persons always receive a *different* treatment such that we always are faced with a comparison of program variations; it is not usually possible to arrange to study a representative sampling of treatments, and though we may be able to generalize about subjects we cannot then generalize about treatment; and it is usually not administratively feasible to test, in a single agency, more than a few varieties of treatment by means of this kind of research design.

Correlational studies can provide the basis for a systematic study of experience, with different classifications of persons, with varieties of treatment, in affecting various outcomes. Thus, the variation in outcomes can be analyzed in terms of components: that due to characteristics of the persons classed as offenders, to program variation, and to error. Through the use of a variety of multivariate designs, statistical controls can to some extent be substituted for the lacking experimental controls; and, when the null hypothesis for treatment effects fails to be supported, further research using experimental designs might then be developed in order to test hypotheses about the source of the difference.

Such an approach can provide tools for analyses of decisions concerning persons involved with the criminal justice system—from arrest to final discharge—and can point the way to a better investment of time when classical experimental designs are used. Given an adequate information system, with reliable information on persons, treatments, and outcomes, the large-scale use of multivariate methods in this way is now completely feasible due to the increased availability of high speed computers. This can enable us to survey the terrain to identify where oil is more likely to be found; then we can dig deeper there.

Thus, it may be proposed that "the two disciplines of scientific psychology" can provide the framework for meeting the fourth challenge— that of monitoring corrections' ability to achieve its goals. Needed in each social agency responsible for crime and delinquency treatment and control programs is an information base permitting study of the natural variation in management information on program effectiveness and useful guides to further, more rigorous and more detailed research.

An important feature of such a monitoring system is found in prediction methods, which provide useful tools for program evaluation studies by identifying and summarizing variables which must be controlled, either statistically or experimentally, when groups are to be compared. Consideration of the prediction problem again confronts us with a vast literature; but a number of critical research problems may be abstracted from a recent review (Gottfredson, 1966):

1. Improvement of the criterion measures of delinquency or crime to be predicted.

2. Cross-validation studies of available measures in order to test their applicability in various jurisdictions, and repeated assessment of validity along with social change.

3. Development of prediction measures for specific subgroups, rather than for samples of total populations of children or of adults.

4. Empirical comparisons of various methods in use for combining predictors.

40   5. Systematic follow up from studies demonstrating a variety of discriminators of "delinquent" and "non-delinquent" samples in order to improve current prediction methods.
6. Improvement of statistical prediction methods by testing hypotheses from clinical practice.
7. Utilization of mathematical decision theory, including attention to assessment of the social and monetary costs associated with errors and successes along the correctional continuum.
8. Building prediction methods into the information system of each agency responsible for the custody, treatment, or release of persons accused or convicted of law-violations in order to permit repeated validation studies, provide systematic feedback to decision-makers, and provide tools for program evaluations.

THE NEED FOR RESEARCH UTILIZATION

The gap between what is known and what is applied is often discussed, but seldom has it been recognized as a problem worthy of study in its own right; and the fifth major challenge confronting correctional psychology is to develop and test ways to ensure communication and utilization of research results. Research aimed specifically at understanding the processes by which research results can be incorporated to modify existing programs, or lead to new ones, is needed. Related studies are needed to point the ways in which knowledge gained from psychological research can influence public understanding and public policy concerning the prevention, treatment, and control of delinquency and crime.

While a lack of utilization of research is much decried, one may wonder whether that lack itself has been well demonstrated; perhaps more research is used than is realized. In designing new correctional programs, for example, does not the whole "apperceptive mass" of those involved come into play? Do correctional administrators, like Tolman's rats, exhibit latent learning? Would token economies be developing in prisons except for Skinner, or indeed, for Hull, or Thorndike? Would the present emphasis on increased use of alternatives to incarceration be maintained in the absence of demonstrations that such alternatives can be used without increased public risk, or of repeated failures to demonstrate rehabilitative gains due to confinement? Would the prison pendulum have swung from revenge to restraint to rehabilitation to reintegration in the community without the input of social science?

There is not increased funding of demonstration projects, however, and with that is a greater responsibility of guarding against the danger—so often seen in the past—of programs ending when the project period is over and the research pulls out. The need is great for well planned and programmed implementation of the project results. For such implementation to occur, a

monitoring function, a questioning attitude, and an institutionalization of data   41
collection and processing functions—all must be built into the agency itself
in the course of the project. In order for this to take place, agency staff, and
not just the researchers, need to be involved in, and a part of, the whole
process. If *A* is to learn from *B*, it has to be *B*'s thing. For many projects, as
much attention should be given to the development and follow through of an
implementation model as for the research itself. The aim should be to
implant within the agency a repetitive cycle, as a continuity of effort, of
questioning, research, demonstration, system modification, and more questioning. Administrators must begin to ask, How do you know?, and to act on the
basis of the present evidence, then to question the new procedures.

THE PSYCHOLOGISTS' ROLE

Psychologists will, I believe, see outstanding opportunities for their
best skills in meeting these challenges. Jacques Loeb, asked whether he was a
philosopher, psychologist, chemist, neurologist, or physicist, replied, "I
solve problems [Maslow, 1954]." Solving problems which are primarily
behavioral is the business of psychologists, and the problems which must be
solved in order to cope more rationally, efficiently, and humanely with
delinquency and crime are mainly behavioral. Psychologists of various incli-
nations, in collaboration with others, will be needed to meet the five challenges
described: to develop an integrated theoretical framework, to define person
classifications with demonstrable relevance to treatment alternatives, to
develop new treatment and control strategies and test their effectiveness, to
develop—in every social agency responsible for crime and delinquency
programs—adequate information bases to permit the monitoring of program
effectiveness, and to devise effective means for research utilization.

Responsibilities, Commitments and Roles

4

"The psychologist always finds that he must consider his loyalties to his 'clients' and to his institution, for often they conflict [Corsini, 1945]."

There are many skills and knowledge areas that mental health professionals and behavioral scientists bring to justice agencies. The responsibilities and roles they assume depend in part upon these abilities, the requirements of the position, and the characteristics of the agency. Within these limitations, there are varying responsibilities and roles defined by the professional himself. Most behavioral scientists assume multiple roles and functions in almost every facet of justice system involvement—planning, direct service, consultation, research. Issues of community protection, morale of agency employees, welfare of some client group, general professional ethics, public relations and effectiveness of the agency also delimit his role.

The overlapping roles and the varying definitions of "client" (the agency, the offender, the community) are frequently sources of personal and professional conflict. This struggle is reflected in the description by Raymond Corsini (1945) of his work as a psychologist at San Quentin. He complained of role conflict arising in part from "professional isolation . . . in a hostile or at least suspicious environment . . . [with] petty intrigues, unbending discipline, chicanery, deadening routine, and the general attitude of defeat." All of these depressing characteristics may or may not be present in any given justice agency, but the situation often does exist in which there are competing objectives and incompatible demands.

This role conflict takes place on a number of decision levels. At one level, it takes the form of deciding which alternative is actually best for the client. At another, it is deciding which of the clientele groups should be served. And at a third level, it is resolving conflicts between organizational client expectations, and appropriate professional behavior.

These problems vary in scope and intensity, depending upon the agency goals and the professional's function and role, but the conflict is basic and pervasive.

The responsibilities, roles, and applications of psychology and other behavioral sciences may be viewed in terms of divergent commitments, ranging from "system-professional" to "system-challenger." This continuum, of course, covers a broad range of activities and views.

A system-professional commitment suggests an acceptance of many existing professional procedures and objectives. While there may be disagreements about the quantity or quality of psychological or behavioral science applications, there is substantial agreement with existing targets of professional involvement and patterns of belief. On the other hand, persons at the system-challenger end of the continuum suggest that existing functions and loyalties are unjustified or otherwise problematic, and raise questions about the desirability of achieving many of the specified objectives. Published expressions of this latter view are found in the journal, *Radical Therapist*, and in the book, *Struggle For Justice* (American Friends Service Committee, 1971).

The system-professional/system-challenger issue will be described with respect to four areas of responsibility. The middle points, as well as the points at either end of the continuum, will be identified.

RESPONSIBILITIES TO THE OFFENDER AS RECIPIENT OF DIRECT CLINICAL SERVICES

System-Professional

A mental health professional view is that society has a responsibility to change the negative psychological functioning of the offender-client through meaningful rehabilitative or "habilitative" programs. (See Chapter 6 for a research perspective on this approach.)

Typically, a tenet of this position is that justice agency policies which seek to change behavior through punishment or intimidation are ineffective in the long run. Rather, offenders need to develop strong internal control that will result in societally appropriate behavior. Thus Menninger (1968) sees the criminal as "a person who for all sorts of reasons is chronically and basically more uncomfortable than most of us," and whose "constitutional method of dealing with his discomfort is by direct actions." If Menninger's belief that "self-control is mental health" is accepted, the professional's responsibility to the offender-client is to aid him in developing more self-control. One of the variety of ways to meet this responsibility is by setting up situations and pressures that prompt offender clients to become motivated to change— typically through counseling and psychotherapy. The commitment to the client is to help him repress his criminogenic tendencies through planning and implementation of individualized treatment programs.

System-Challenger

Those at the system-challenging end of the continuum hold that such "Menningerian" thinking leads to indeterminate sentences and devices intended to coerce the client into treatment. This coercion is seen as leading to more subtle and even more punitive consequences. The social injustices of poverty, discrimination, selective law-enforcement, and unfair judicial actions, are perceived as the core problems, rather than the criminal being behaviorally deviant and in need of treatment. In a discussion of the "Crime of Treatment" the American Friends Service Committee (AFSC) (1971) stated:

> Most inmates participate in these (group counseling) sessions only because they feel they have to. They lack commitment and are fearful that anything meaningful revealed in these sessions might be used against them and damage their chances of receiving a parole. Consequently, the sessions seldom move beyond the bland and the trivial.

As an alternate proposal, the AFSC proposed that *fully voluntary* clinical and therapeutic services be offered free to the entire population, both those connected with the justice system and persons apart from it. Any imposition of services is seen as a type of "blackmail" with sentence length as the bargaining lever.

> There is a belief held by many, especially experts in the social service fields, that lower-class, emotionally disturbed, "deviant" or "criminal" persons most often are not aware of their real problems and will not seek services that can help them. We disagree totally with this proposition. In the first place, help must be defined from the viewpoint of the person in need, and in the second place, the reason a person in need turns his back on help is, by and large, that the services offered are shabby substitutes for help. When real services are available, those in need literally line up at the door [American Friends Service Committee, 1971].

Midpoints and Cautions

The description of these dichotomous views does not imply that there are no mid-points. Indeed a common professional perspective may combine these two views. Adherents to the intermediary position feel that a structure which requires clinical participation is necessary for certain types of clients, and is altogether inappropriate for others.

In a discussion of direct services to the client, it should be remembered that many professionals fulfill their responsibilities to their clients through indirect services, such as system changes, policy level decisions, planning, and consultation. In this latter context, some first-hand knowledge of the clientele (e.g., through direct services or experience), builds a base for establishing credibility and success.

RESPONSIBILITIES TO THE AGENCY

System-Professional

The system-professional goals within the agency are agency effectiveness, appropriate professional input to the agency and acceptance of recommendations at policy levels. As stated elsewhere in this report, defining organizational objectives in clearly specified terms so that they can be achieved is extremely important. A necessary first step is to develop credibility. This means speaking with people, rather than telling them what to do. It means building good working relationships within the agency. It means giving administrators a sense that one is clearly on their side, and not an opponent. It means asking what one can do to help the individual achieve what he wants to achieve. And finally, it means developing a sense of confidence and mutual respect so that one is asked the questions one wants to answer.

From this view, loyalties and mutual commitments between mental health professionals and justice agency administrators are often characterized by bad faith. The agency, desperate for mental health workers, hires psychologists and others who are minimally qualified. Not infrequently there are bachelor degree graduates working in psychologist's positions, who are familiar with neither the relevant literature nor the basic skills for job-appropriate behavior. A solution to this particular problem is an immediate upgrading of personnel standards and the hiring of qualified, interested graduates of Masters and PhD level programs.

For new personnel as well as those currently within the system, one route to becoming an effective change agent is to establish mutual confidence and good will relationships. There is a need for both psychological personnel and agency administrators to say to each other, "I believe in you as an individual and professional and I believe you should be here." Such an attitude does not emerge in a vacuum, however. It is closely related to one's philosophy concerning clients and role-definitions. Principles of communication that enhance this good will process include modeling listening behavior, getting feedback that one is hearing accurately, avoiding listening only to people that reflect one's own perspective.

When these favorable conditions prevail, the behavioral scientist may have a large amount of system input. It has been suggested that behavioral scientists in justice agencies really don't know their potential strength. To cite examples of effective change agents, Fenton and Warren in California, as well as Levinson and Quay in the Federal Bureau of Prisons, have influenced the operating philosophies and functioning of their respective cor- rectional agencies.[4]

System-Challenger

The system-challenging view is that of the outside critic who believes that active participants in an agency or system become part of it, indiscriminately adopting its implicit values and goals. "The experts—even the most enlightened and progressive—also line up solidly in support of the system, asking only for more of the same [American Friends Service Committee, 1971]." This process is not necessarily rational and conscious, but is part of a "It never happened and besides they deserved it" double-think that overlooks and denies agency errors and wrong-doing (Opton, 1971). Another part of this threat is the potential loss of scientific and professional perspective and imagination through inclusion in the administration hierarchy.

From this perspective, the danger is felt to be that the professional will become more concerned with what is best for the staff and the agency (often in a Parkinson's Law sense) than in what is best for the client. The professional adheres to the old proverb, "Whose bread I eat, his song I sing." Loyalties to the "boss" may lead to questionable professional activities, such as slanting research results (perhaps through deceptive tables or charts), or taking client-related actions for political purposes or in-house expediency.

The system-professional adherent might work with an agency to lessen intra-agency tension through developing programs to release individual and group expressions of distress. The system-challenger might suggest that the tension should remain until its causes are removed; the underlying premise is that tension is an appropriate signal that ought to be heard and dealt with, not muted.

A system-challenger assumption is that negative, harmful activities are perpetrated by justice agencies. Thus the professional's role should be as system or agency skeptic for these settings that have poorly implemented but reasonable objectives, and system sabateur in "harmful" agencies. Howard and Somers (1971) have described the pertinent process of resisting institutional evil from within. Directing their attention to institutions that dehumanize others, they point out:

> Among the hazards for the anticipatory resister is the fact that insiders are treated as insiders and begin to define themselves accordingly. Other factors equal, the longer one participates in evil, the greater his chance of being demoralized, co-opted, and rendered incapable of severing his connection with the institution.

---

[4]The specific influences are by Norman Fenton in promoting group counseling programs, by Marguerite Warren in developing the Community Treatment and Differential Treatment projects, and by Robert Levinson and Herbert Quay in designing the behavior research-treatment programs at the Kennedy Youth Center, Morgantown, West Virginia.

Howard and Somers suggest that system resisters may retain their values and integrity by acting as counter-organizers, resisters, or disrupters.

Midpoints

While the methods of change as well as views of justice institutions are at disparate positions on the continuum, the theoretical gap is much greater than observable differences for some participants. If some agreement is reached that the mutual purposes are to improve justice agencies, it would be quite possible to see identical professional or scientist behavior for very different reasons. Perhaps some optimal point would be found in the person who has the clout and credibility of the system-professional and the indignation and dissatisfaction of the system-challenger.

RESPONSIBILITIES TO SELF AND PROFESSION

System-Professional

In this report, Judge Bazelon raises the question of whether psychologists and other behavioral scientists in justice agencies are "doing good for offenders or well for themselves?" The system professional response to that query is, "Both!" Activities in which desired objectives are achieved quite properly reflect well on those behavioral scientists involved. The question then is moot, since professional and personal gain accompanies "doing good for offenders." The actual definition of what *is* "doing good" is more troublesome. One answer is that "good" programs and involvement arise out of no single orthodoxy in justice agencies. Consequently professional and scientific activities are constrained only by conformity to accepted disciplinary norms and ethical standards.

System-Challenger

The system-challenger perspective is based on the observation that no professional, personal, or agency activity can ever be value-free. The most scientific and objective appearing findings or programs may have subjective and non-rational elements. Some activities are truly carried out in one's own personal or professional interest and one should be aware of this. Behavioral science value systems often will differ from those of justice agencies and administrators. Recommendations for action will be, and ought to be, developed from these values rather than exclusively from scientific information. Some contend that such values must be made explicit. They define the role of the behavioral scientist as coming from a "biased objectivity."

RESPONSIBILITY TO SOCIETY

System-Professional

The system-professional perspective is that it is important to "do the

do-able." Because behavioral scientists and mental health professionals have
little control over societal decisions and actions, what can be done must lie
within the existing field of both job and client. Broader societal issues relating
to deviance, for example, are important insofar as they are relevant to professional behaviors. This view would hold that the offender has placed himself under the care and control of the larger community by virtue of his
law-violation. Society has a responsibility to protect itself and therefore is
entitled to take such actions and provide such treatment that would prevent
future antisocial behavior. The responsibility of the mental health professional
is not to act as social critic, but rather to deal with these offenders as well as
he can with the joint interests of the offender and society considered.

System-Challenger

The point of view perpetrated by the system-challenger is that scientists
and professionals typically have "discipline-centric" myopia, and are never
able to pull back from their immediate functions to look at justice systems
more broadly. Such individuals become the equivalent of World War II "Good
Germans," not questioning the practices or assumptions of dealing with problems of social deviance. Their narrow preoccupation with scientific roles and
functions makes professionals insensitive to the larger social issues.

There are many direct implications of the system-challenger social-activ-
ist position. Typically, they take the form of programs that divert people
from the justice system, increase legal and group tolerance for deviance, and
diminish the use of the juvenile and criminal justice systems to solve social
problems. The American Friends Service Committee (1971) states concisely
one of its major goals: "Getting the justice system off our backs."

SUMMARY AND CONCLUSIONS

A colleague, who had just finished sitting through two days of discussion
at the Lake Wales meetings about responsibilities and roles without saying
anything, finally reported with puzzlement and frustration that these role-
conflicts really did not apply to him. However, he worked in an unusual agency
and had defined for himself a largely conflict-free role.

There are a few professionals who are not caught up in these issues and
still others who although involved, are not fully aware of the problems. Some
behavioral scientists have entered the justice system with a role definition
that reduces conflict. Examples of these are the police department and the
court clinic psychologists. It would appear that the explicit definition of
responsibilities, scope and agency loyalties relieves some of the subjective
discomfort of the professionals involved.

Nevertheless, the issue of role-conflict may be examined with respect to
any justice agency employee. The resolution of the issue may rest with the

50 extent to which the individual concerns himself with limited, clearly defined behaviors, or seeks to be involved at broader, societal levels.

The development of this continuum of system-professional to system-challenger attitudes oversimplifies a very complex phenomenon. One hazard is the stereotypic, good-guy/bad guy thinking that is associated with one's identification with any single point of view. Individuals should be able to see themselves as pursuing multiple goals and commitments simultaneously. There is no reason for justice to be a zero sum game, with society's gain arising at the expense of the convicted person, or vice-versa.

Commitments and perceived responsibilities are related to effectiveness in changing justice agencies. The white-coated psychotherapist, sitting in his leather-upholstered, tilt-back, swivel chair, and seeing offender-clients all day, has limited opportunity to influence a system. Similarly the fiery radical whose immediate concern is to liberate a few prisons has little probability of success. Among the many professionals in-between are those who can mentally step outside the system to gain objectivity, and yet remain within it. This combined role of the conceptualizer, who is aware of organizational structure, as well as the participant, who is not co-opted, offers considerable promise for affecting agencies and having impact.

How does a professional get to this point? Who defines what he does? Is it a matter of the agency establishing performance standards to which the professional must either measure up or get out? Or, do the professional and his discipline establish the standard to which the agency must comply?

There is another alternative. The professional defines himself, taking into consideration both his agency's demands and his discipline's ethics. In a variety of ways, the psychologist in a justice agency establishes the outside limits within which he is more or less free to function. The degree of freedom will vary depending upon the flexibility of administrative policy. The maximum use of this freedom will depend on the skills, capabilities, and beliefs of the individual involved. Perhaps all the faults do not lie within the stars.

The Psychologist as Action Researcher

Marguerite Q. Warren

This chapter focuses on the psychologist as an action researcher in the criminal justice area. The last decade has seen an increasing number of action research projects being conducted, especially in the field of corrections. Much of this research has been the work of psychologists. By and large, this is not research about the criminal justice system conducted in academic settings, but rather research conducted in operating agencies with all its real-life complexities.

One appropriate role for the psychologist involved in action research is the development of the action *program* in such a way that it can be adequately researched; i.e., providing easy availability of information on clients, staff and program elements; a clear conceptualization of the program's goals, hypotheses, and anticipated outcomes; and an atmosphere of openness to inquiry encouraged throughout the program. Although a psychologist can be seen as very appropriate for this program development role, perhaps an even more important contribution can be made by the psychologist operating on the *research* side of the action research effort. While individuals with clinical skills, but without research know-how, can play the program development role, the psychologist with a combination of clinical and research training appears uniquely qualified to carry out the action research role.

The psychologist's role as action researcher can be described in terms of a number of major functions which relate to different stages of project development: (*a*) getting the research project designed and the design approved

52   by program administrators, program developers and implementers; (b) getting an action program of high quality (i.e., worth researching) conceptualized, planned, implemented, and monitored; (c) describing the program processes, building and testing hypotheses, and evaluating program impact; and (d) utilizing research findings to encourage social agency change.

The first stage, getting the research project designed and agreed upon by all participants, involves a function requiring all of the psychologist's inter-personal skills, as well as his scientific capabilities. The interpersonal skills are crucial because the action researcher must really be able to hear where the program people are—their needs, motives, beliefs (explicit and implicit) and priorities, in order to communicate what the research is likely to do and not to do in relation to those needs, beliefs and priorities. The researcher must, in this dialogue, be able to assure himself that any experimental design involved will not be violated. The assurance of support for "research integrity" at both top and middle management levels is crucial. This support will undoubt-edly be tested during the life of the project, so that lip-service support will not suffice. In order to guarantee the design, the researcher should have a direct line communication channel to the level of administration responsible for final decisions. In effect, the agency must be encouraged to think of its experimental programs in a social laboratory light. Respect and status for the agency must result from the willingness to assess a program rather than from the illusion of an infallible program. Administrators must understand that, in the field's present state of knowledge, the risk of negative or inconclusive findings is certainly present. Warnings must also be given to agency admin-istrators regarding the extent to which the experimental program is likely to interfere with "normal operations." Strains on the agency's policies, proce-dures and organizational structure, as well as demands for an unusual level of financial support, decentralized autonomy, etc., must be presented as realistically as available data will permit. Faced with this warning concerning potential implementation strains, one may wonder whether an agency admin-istrator will agree to innovate—particularly without being guaranteed that such programs will have payoff for his agency.

Likely payoff for the agency can be presented to the administrator without guaranteeing results. Examples may be given of governmental agencies which have gained considerable positive feedback nationally for their willing-ness to experiment. A pilot project may be recommended and the advantages pointed out—advantages which include the delaying of a broad implementa-tion in the agency until some outcome data are available. The advantages of being able to decide about future program development on the basis of scientific knowledge, rather than on the enthusiasm of individuals in the agency, can be noted. Payoff in the form of agency self-study, with its requirement of increased conceptualization of goals and procedures for reaching them, can be pointed out as a staff training method. And, finally, the possibility of finding improved methods of carrying out the agency's mandate is probably the most convincing of all potential payoffs for the administrators.

A research matter to be explored in this beginning stage by the researcher is whether or not the agency is willing to permit a random assignment procedure, either to an experimental and a control group or to two or more experimental conditions. The major staff argument against random assignment procedures involves a belief that program staff already know what will be effective, or can already identify those clients who are, for example, most "amenable" to the proposed action program, and that thus depriving some "amenable" individuals of the program, represents an injustice. The researcher can point out that if our state of knowledge is of such an order, the experiment need not be run. If however the true state of affairs is that, while staff have hypotheses about program impact, they do not have certain knowledge, the experiment will either verify the hypotheses or suggest alternates. Threat to the agency's current program can be reduced by suggesting that the experimental design need not be aimed at proving that the innovative procedures are superior to the old program, but that the design can ask which clients are benefited by the new program and which by the old.

If random assignment of clients to programs is approved, the researcher will be faced with deciding whether to utilize an experimental/control (E/C) design or an experimental/experimental (E/E) design. There are several difficulties with the more scientifically-respectable experimental/control design in an action setting. The first involves the difficulty of *controlling* variables within complex action programs. Ideally in the E/C model, the experimental subjects will receive certain special "treatment" or innovative elements, and the control subjects will receive "nothing." However, in almost all projects in the criminal justice area, the control subjects in fact receive "something else"—presumed not to be so beneficial as the experimental intervention. What control status frequently means is simply that the experimenter does not know precisely what happens to these cases other than intake and outcome data. While the intervening experiences may be well described for the experimental cases, experiences for the controls—which may be just as impactful—are simply unknown. For those projects in which control status does not clearly represent an *absence* of something but a *presence* of something else, it would appear that an E/E design is a better alternative.

The Hawthorne effect resulting from the extra attention given the experimental subjects and staff is an often-noted second difficulty with the E/C design in action research. A further difficulty which is almost impossible to avoid in action programs is the possibility of differential decisions being made on experimental and control subjects to the advantage of one group or the other. It is a rare situation in which the decision-makers on individual clients do not know the prior program experience of those clients. In this case not only may program biases in favor of the experimental or control program lead

54 to differential decisions, but also the very fact that more extensive information is available on experimental cases, may bias the decisions.

In contrast to the *E/C* design, the *E/E* design sets two innovative programs into action, both believed by their respective proponents to offer promise of more favorable outcome than the usual or regular agency program. The argument against the *E/E* design is that one will not find out whether "nothing" is as good as or better than either experimental program. Perhaps it can be argued that especially in the corrections area of the criminal justice field, the alternative of "nothing" has often been tried and the record speaks for itself. The advantages of the *E/E* design are many. With respect to action aspects, one may hope to equalize staff investment in outcome, motivation to succeed, dedication which shows up in extra hours of duty, willingness to accept middle-of-the-night and weekend calls of distress, and so forth. Also in the program area, one can hope to equalize the resources (e.g., training funds, consultation) available from the parent agency of the study to carry out the intent of the experiment. One may also equalize freedom from the usual constraints on operation imposed by the agency in the form of paper work, higher echelon permission for case decisions and other "red tape."

An advantage of the *E/E* model over the *E/C* model for research purposes involves both the extent and the accuracy of information collected on experimental cases compared to control cases. An additional advantage for research lies in the effort made to describe the process of treatment in both programs, rather than having to compare a known program with an unknown program. If the data show one subgroup of the population "doing better" in one of the two experimental programs, the researcher has a much more solid data base on which to hypothesize the reasons. When a subgroup shows up "doing better" in a control group, speculation as to reasons is likely to be based on very little data.

These are examples of the kinds of issues the action researcher will be struggling with at the project's beginning. They represent an argument for the combination of interpersonal and scientific skills the action researcher needs to possess.

The functioning of the psychologist as action researcher in the second stage of project development, involves working with the action staff involved in the project to increase the level of conceptualization of program specifics. Specifically, what will be done with what kinds of clients, by what kinds of workers, in what kinds of settings? On what basis are specific program elements assumed to interact with what aspects of clients or their environment in order to achieve what goals? The role of the action researcher in this conceptualization process is extremely important. Through use of intelligent questions, the researcher can encourage greater specificity with respect to the nature of the problems to be dealt with, the program goals pertaining to those problems, the methods of reaching those goals, and definitions of criteria of progress toward

goals. The researcher can use his conceptual skills to move the intervention
program to the level of a *model* which can be subsequently applied by others.

The researcher can help action staff decide the extent to which they will ask to be seen by their agency in a "special" light, by requesting a pick of experienced staff, a higher-than-typical salary range, special operating freedom for the staff, special organizational structure—all in the belief that these factors may contribute significantly to program success. Or, the researcher may help the staff determine the extent to which they will attempt to operate within the usual agency mold. For the researcher, the issue of generalizability of findings is at stake, as well as the issue of utilization of research findings in program expansion. While there is not an obvious answer to the issue of "specialness," the action researcher's role is to help staff become aware of the implications of choosing one path or the other.

The monitoring function—keeping the program moving toward its specified goals, using only specified program elements—is in part a responsibility of the action researcher. This function may be carried out in a variety of ways, but is certain to involve an open interchange between action staff and researcher around the ongoing process of building intervention strategies, identifying where the planned program is and is not being carried out, and revising strategy when necessary. Some experience in action research programs has given considerable support to the position that researchers who have direct and frequent contact with action personnel—and with study subjects— will be in an unusually good position to develop the detailed knowledge which must underlie any comprehensive intervention model statements. This type of research involvement seems to increase the likelihood of learning perhaps as much from so-called program failures as from so-called program successes— since in the former case action staff will usually be more willing to speak candidly when long-term relationships exist with research staff.

An additional point is that an interested listener is crucial to adequate intervention reporting. When asking workers in the human services what is appealing about their jobs, one often hears positive comments about their independence from supervision. This sometimes has the "sweet lemon" quality of the worker identifying as a blessing, a typical lack of supervision for workers in case management jobs. In contrast, one hears staff in an action research project demanding and thriving on feedback obtained from intervention supervisors and researchers. Motivation is high where a researcher not only hears the worker describe his efforts and the problems faced and overcome, but even "takes notes" about it.

On the other hand, ongoing contact with action personnel places research in a very complicated role—one which must be handled with considerable care. The researcher must, after all, maintain his perspective of objectivity. Because of the concern with objectivity, some researchers have preferred to think of themselves as "in-house skeptics." This term is a bothersome one. While it must be clear that the researcher will be convinced, not by staff enthusiasm, but only by objective data, the term "skeptic" can be expected to put action staff on the defensive thus reducing the likelihood of open communication about program. The fear of action researchers about contaminating their data by getting too close to the subjects of their study, can lead to never finding out what is really going on in the intervention process. A more satisfactory description of the action researcher involves the role of searcher for truth whose training has prepared him to understand the nature of evidence.

Much of the process-oriented research in an action program can be conducted in connection with ongoing project activities. For example, recording for research purposes can be set up so that it does not add to, but rather substitutes for the usual reports demanded by the agency. If a group intervention activity is being evaluated by staff or if an individual case staffing is being conducted, the researcher can act as recorder as well as a source for conceptualization.

It is obvious that again in this second function of the researcher, both the interpersonal skills and the scientific capabilities of the psychologist are needed.

With respect to the third stage or function, that of program description and impact evaluation, the psychologist willing to work in an action research area has indicated his willingness to collect data in all its real-life complexity. Although he will, of course, attempt to obtain all of the hard data available with respect to outcome measures and pre-post change, it is likely that in the area of process-oriented exploratory research the most useful insights will be obtained. It is a rare project in which process research consists of other than "clinical" data. The exciting aspect of clinical data is that the researcher is hopeful of getting close to the real thing; i.e., the "thing" that is actually going on, which is aimed at having therapeutic or other defined consequences. The problem is that clinical data is "messy" data; i.e., it possesses all the faults of complexity, subjectivity and "unaccountability." It doesn't come in neat categories; it requires interpretation. Everything is interactive with everything else. And because of all these difficulties, it almost defies that most respectable of scientific procedures—hypothesis testing.

Without minimizing the research difficulties in this situation, it may be suggested that the worst sin of all is over-simplification. The research task must be begun at a level of complexity sufficient to accommodate all the data which appears to be realistically relevant. Not only are the numbers of dimensions, variables, conditions, levels and combinations exceedingly large, but also all of these may be variable with kind of client, kind of staff, time period, etc. Data are available in some research projects which show the distorted nature of data produced when any of these crucial dimensions are ignored. The complexity is increased when one considers that *measures* of preferred *outcome* may also be variable depending on the nature of the client and/or his problem. For example, in identifying hoped-for changes in individual offenders following a correctional treatment program, one may say that increased signs of conformity are a positive sign in a psychopathic person, but have negative meaning in a conformist whose delinquency results from overcompliance to delinquent peers. In other words, differential predictions must be made with regard to signs of improvement in different types of cases.

Although it is obvious that successful outcome must be measured using a range of criteria, since no known single criterion is completely satisfactory, the researcher will still be faced with establishing a hierarchy of preferred alternatives. If a youth stops stealing cars, but gets permanently expelled from school because of smoking on the school yard, is he getting better or worse? A theoretical framework will, of course, help order the data. However, at the level of data collection, itself, it seems important to record as completely as possible, the data which are seen as relevant by the subject, the worker and the observer—within theoretically defined cateogries where possible. Moving from the raw data to condensed but meaningful documents is a monumental task. On the other hand, to record at this point only the data for which pre-established categories of analysis are available, means the loss of the complexity required to be anywhere close to reality. Again, the psychologist with some theoretical training in his background may be in the best position to make sense out of this data complexity.

While *process* data is admittedly on the "soft" side, it is assumed that *outcome* data should be hard data. Yet, it is extremely difficult to find a criterion which cannot be criticized on the basis of the subjective judgments going into it. Researchers in the criminal justice area are often told that they are in a much better position than researchers in other social problem areas because they have a hard criterion such as recidivism with which to judge their programs. However, recidivism data have long been challenged with respect to the subjectivity going into these decisions. Good and bad discharges from correctional agencies, arrests, parole suspensions, court verdicts, are all criteria which may be criticized on the same basis. Getting and holding jobs, remaining in school, are also criteria which are subject to numerous and unknown influences aside from the behavior of the subject. This is not a comforting picture but one which the action researcher must face. The creative researcher will combine these pseudo-hard data with the even-less-hard data of reports from clients and workers in order to tease out the best evidence of what is happening.

A strong case can be made in conducting research in the criminal justice area for use of a classification system of offenders. Although it is generally accepted that an offender population is a heterogeneous one in terms of the variety of patterns by which individuals get into a correctional system, much research has been done without utilizing a classification of this heterogeneous population. It is possible in a number of studies to show that if one omits a classification breakdown of the offender population, one can *conceal* dramatic differences among offenders in the outcome of treatment programs. A psychologist is perhaps in as good a position, or better, than most other social scientists to be aware of and to take into consideration a classificatory breakdown of the offender population.

With respect to the fourth stage of function, utilizing research findings to encourage social agency change, two aspects can be discussed: (*a*) the transfer of a successful program to another agency or another part of the agency, and (*b*) the broader impact on the agency of increased program conceptualization. A frequently-heard lament of agencies which fund innovative programs in criminal justice, concerns the speed with which successful programs disappear when the research phase is over. A number of factors already mentioned or implied in this chapter may help account for this phenomenon. The program may well have created strains on the usual operating procedures and the risk level of the agency, along with some resentment from those parts of the agency not directly involved with the project. Clues about resentment appear in such comments as: "All the resources of this agency have been going to that unit for *too* long." "We could do just as well if *we* had low caseloads and the pick of staff." "That program is so fancy, it could never be replicated." "And in walked the project staff, all with their pipes and their horn-rimmed glasses." In addition to feelings of resentment, non-project staff may well feel defensive of their programs which have come out second-best in the data analysis. Such feelings may lead administration to cancel the program for "staff morale purposes." A further force to close the program may arise from the agency's having innovated beyond the comfort level of administrators because of the pressure of outside money.

The resentments, which are perhaps inevitable, can be reduced in a number of ways, thus making program survival, as well as expansion, more likely. If the project can function—even with extra difficulty—within the line organization of the agency rather than being assigned to a special division (such as a division of Experimental Programs), it is more likely that the line staff will come to think of the program as their own. Feedback about the impact of specific program elements which could be utilized in the regular operation, can be given with minimum delay after the data are in, so that the charge of secrecy will not be made. Project staff may be able to provide a training or consultation service to the regular program, thus passing along any new skills which will not interfere with the research design.

Rather than a successful innovative project being transferred in toto, more often pieces of the program are picked up by other agencies. Guided Group Interaction programs are found in a wide range of agencies, but without many of the aspects of the original Highfields Project. The Differential Treatment Model, a classification of nine delinquent types and corollary intervention strategies, is being used in a number of correctional agencies but without many elements of the Community Treatment Project, in which the Model was developed. A program need not be transferred in its entirety for research utilization to occur. In fact, these partial transfers may provide additional knowledge, if continued research can, in this way, identify the contribution to success or lack of it, made by program method, for example, versus program setting or other elements.

To the topic of program transfer, it may be worth adding the thought that the research element itself may be a major factor in assuring program expansion. That is, an ongoing research effort can provide an atmosphere in which a second experiment grows logically out of the leads of the first, and the third out of the leads of the second. To the extent that criminal justice agencies can provide built-in evaluation capacity as an assumed aspect of all program development, the numberous benefits which action research can provide may solve not only the transfer problem, but also produce a cumulative fund of scientific and program knowledge.

On the broader issue of bringing about social agency change through action research, it is clear that the processes instituted, such as greater conceptualization of goals and plans, and systematic monitoring, are procedures which can result in a whole agency's becoming more goal-oriented and more rational in their efforts to move toward their goals. Additionally, an agency which has survived its first action research program now has added capabilities both with respect to innovative operations and with respect to action research—both of these available for further pilot efforts. And, in developing this staff potential, a creative force for social agency change is now available *within* the agency—a condition more likely to lead to program improvement than pressure for change coming from outside the agency.

This chapter has suggested that in four stages of an action research project the psychologist has important functions to carry out. These four functions involve: (a) getting the research design developed and accepted; (b) helping to get the action program conceptualized, implemented and monitored; (c) describing the program and evaluating impact; and (d) utilizing the action research to encourage social agency change. It was further suggested that psychologists, with their combination of clinical skill and research training, are uniquely qualified to fulfill the action research role.

Clinical Models and Assumptions

6

The conceptions of delinquency causation extend along a continuum, marked at one extreme by a model restricted to intrapsychic factors, and at the other extreme, by a model limited to environmental and social determinants. In this chapter, the search for largely internal, intrapsychic causes will be examined. Many mental health professionals have conceived of criminality from this perspective in the past. While there are a few who do continue to see mental illness as the root of all crime, the number who do hold this view is considerably less than that imagined by those colleagues in other disciplines and professions who think of mental health professionals primarily as pathology-attributors.

THE SICKNESS MODEL

One of the major assumptions of the internal-sickness model, is that the commission of a crime is indicative of the offender's psychological maladjustment and of his underlying need for professional psychological attention. A form of circular reasoning is frequently employed in reaching this conclusion. If a person is a law-violator, there must be something wrong with him. Otherwise, he would not have broken the law. But why did he break the law? There must be something the matter with him. What's the matter with him? He broke the law. This kind of simplistic reasoning resembles one of the "knots" of Ronald Laing (1970). In its more normal expression in discussions of

62 impulse control, psychopathy, and character disorders, this circular reasoning attains augmented complexity and apparent respectability. The same assumption may be illustrated in the following faulty syllogism:

1. Most people don't commit crimes.
2. Most people are normal.
3. Therefore, people who commit crimes are not normal.

There is no doubt that there are disturbed persons in need of mental health care among justice clients, just as there are in any large population. The percentage of disturbed persons may be somewhat higher among justice clients than among free citizens, but whether the development of illness in the individual precedes or follows entry into the justice system is unclear. It does appear, however, that the association of psychological problems with criminality has prompted much current public and professional attention toward offender psychology.

Robert Lindner's dramatic report of his treatment of severely troubled offenders, aroused much interest and faith in the psychologist's roles. Two of his clients, described in *The Fifty Minute Hour* (1955), are examples of convincing cases. Similarly, the partially fictionalized accounts in Donald Powell Wilson's *My Six Convicts* (1951), depicted a constructive interplay between the psychologist and offenders in a maximum security prison.

The report of the President's Commission on Law Enforcement and the Administration of Justice, Task Force on Corrections (1967) states:

> Some clinicians view almost all crime as evidence of character disorder and assume that therapy is appropriate for most inmates. The most highly developed psychotherapeutic services, however, such as those in Massachusetts and Wisconsin, report that they give primary attention only to about 10 percent of the institutional population. In youthful, particularly female, populations the estimate of percentages of inmates in need of some form of psychotherapy run from 15 to 50 percent. These are generally inmates with severe personality disturbances.

RATES OF PSYCHOPATHOLOGY

The assessment of the incidence of psychological disturbance in any group has subjective elements. Generally, it may be stated: the coarser the assessment method, the lower the recognized incidence of impairment. Conversely, the finer and the more exhaustive the level of inquiry, the more likely there will be evidence of maladjustment. An example of the latter principle was demonstrated in the Mid-Town Manhattan Study (Srole, Langner, Michael, Opler & Rennie, 1962). In careful, structured interviews of 1,660 New York City residents, at their places of residence, a mild degree of impairment was found in 36% of the subjects, a moderate degree in 22%, and a major psychological impairment in 23% of these people who were "performing adult responsibilities passibly, or better."

The comparative examination of estimates of mental disturbance in

foreign countries and the United States yielded highly varied results (Dohren- 63
wend & Dohrenwend, 1965). The level of development of the country, as
well as the point in time at which the data were collected, strongly influenced
the results. The findings, themselves, indicated mental illness rates from less
than 1% to over 60%. The highest pathology rates were found in recent
studies, and in studies that used direct contacts as sources of information.

RESEARCH IN OFFENDER ASSESSMENT

When basic criminology textbooks, review sources, and general professional statements about offender psychopathology are studied,[5] views on psychopathology in offenders seem to split according to disciplinary affiliation.
Psychiatrists often reported, particularly in early sources, high rates of
psychological illness. Abrahamsen (1952) stated, "in all my experience I
have not been able to find one single offender who did not show some mental
pathology. . . . the 'normal' offender is a myth." Similarly, Karpman (1949)
attributed all criminality to abnormal mental states.

Sociologists point to the fact that the insufficiency of available information makes it unreasonable to conclude that offenders are psychologically
different from non-offenders. Barnes and Teeters (1959) suggest that when all
criminals are considered, those not apprehended as well as those arrested and
convicted, that "the criminal class as a whole is certainly as intelligent and
stable, mentally and emotionally, as the general population."

Two thorough reviews by teams of sociologists have been conducted on
the results of personality-test comparisons between delinquent populations
and control groups of "normals." Schuessler and Cressey (1950) found that
only 47 (or 42%) of 113 studies successfully differentiated between the
2 populations. However, 26 of the 30 instruments utilized had essentially
disappeared from professional use by the time the study appeared in 1950.

Waldo and Dinitz (1967) conducted a similar, but more sophisticated,
study of the same topic. They found significant differences in the predicted directions in 47 of 56 objective tests reviewed, in 6 of 8 per-
formance-test studies, and in 19 of 30 projective-test studies. The Minnesota
Multiphasic Personality Inventory (MMPI) successfully differentiated the
groups in 28 of 29 studies, although the reviewers cautioned against unqual-
ified acceptance of MMPI results. Waldo and Dinitz also found that all 8
studies, which used large samples and also controlled at least some relevant
background variables, revealed significant differences as predicted. Overall, of
94 studies reviewed, 76 (or 81%) found significant differences, 70 in the
predicted directions.

----

[5]The author is indebted to Richard Vandiver for his aid in abstracting the
literature summarized here.

TABLE 4
Studies of Psychiatric Evaluations of Offenders

Source	Population	Diagnosis	Percent
Glueck (1918)	608 Sing Sing Prisoners	Psychotic or mentally deteriorated	12.0
		Normal	41.0
		Mentally retarded	28.1
Overholser (1935)	5,000 felons under Briggs Law in Mass.	Abnormal	15.0
		Normal	85.0
Bromberg & Thompson (1937)	9,958 offenders before Court of General Sessions, New York City	Psychotic	1.5
		Psychoneurotic	6.9
		Psychopathic personalities	6.9
		Feebleminded	2.4
		Normal or mild personality defects	82.3
Schilder (1940)	Convicted felons, Court of General Sessions of New York City	Psychotic	1.6
		Neurotic	4.2
		Psychopathic personalities	7.3
		Feebleminded	3.1
		Normal	83.8
Banay (1941)	Sing Sing prisoners	Psychotic	1.0
		Emotionally immature	20.0
		Psychopathic	17.0
		Normal	62.0
Poindexter (1955)	100 problem inmates	Mentally ill	20.0
		Normal	80.0
Schlessinger & Blau (1957)	500 typical prisoners	Character and behavior disorders	85.0
		Normal	15.0

Source	Population	Diagnosis	Percent
Shands (1958)	1720 North Carolina felon admissions to Central Prison	Psychotic	3.5
		Personality disorder	55.8
		Psychoneurotic	3.9
		Sociopathic personality	7.0
		Other	5.3
		No psychiatric disorder	4.7
		Transient personality disorder	19.8
Brodsky (1970)	32,511 military prisoners	Character and behavior disorders	77.1
		No psychiatric disease	21.3
		Miscellaneous disorders	1.6

66   The diagnostic systems, themselves, are open to critical evaluation. Thus Tappan (1960) remarked that, "figures on psychoneurosis and psychopathic personality are too variable, as are the concepts themselves, to offer much insight into the prevalence of these disorders among criminals." Although there is disagreement among behavioral scientists, there is also much skepticism concerning the unusually high rate of psychological illness attributed to offenders as a group.

Research reports on the psychiatric assessment of offenders have yielded a wide range of results. Table 4 summarizes nine such studies from a research review of offender diagnoses (Brodsky, 1972). Meaningful comparisons between studies are difficult to make because different populations were sampled, because diagnostic categories were dissimilar, and because a time period of over 50 years was represented. Nevertheless, it may be observed that the reported range of psychotic illnesses was quite narrow. The researchers usually found between 1 and 2% of the populations to be psychotic.

The range of findings relating to psychological normality was much broader. Four studies found over 80% of the sampled offenders to be normal (Overholser, 1935; Bromberg & Thompson, 1937; Schilder, 1940; Poindexter, 1955).

Parallel to Dohrenwend and Dohrenwend's (1965) findings, in more recent studies a smaller percentage of those offenders examined were determined to be essentially normal. The reporting of normality, however, is subject to many administrative and non-psychological influences. For example, in the diagnostic system of Illinois, none of the five official categories indicated general well-being or normal adjustment. The most positive of the categories was "no gross personality defects." Given this cautious indication of possible normality, it was applied to less than 2% of the 4,453 prisoners observed in an Illinois diagnostic center (Twomey, 1967).

There is one major limitation on the interpretation of this set of studies and the prior reviews. They all deal with groups of persons who have gone through criminal justice proceedings. There may well be reason to believe that this experience swells the magnitude of existing psychological difficulties and perhaps plants new ones where few had taken root. Thus, Schuessler and Cressey point out that, "the results of this method do not indicate whether criminal behavior is the result of a certain personality trait or whether the trait is the result of criminal experiences."

CONCLUSIONS

The implications of the present review of clinical model assumptions and findings are threefold. First, it is neither reasonable nor appropriate to administer clinical services to justice clients in general. Such blanket treatment is necessarily wasteful and may even lead to iatrogenic pathology. Those clients who resist clinical services are then in danger of being labeled "negativistic" or "undesirables."

Second, it is suggested that there may be a high potential inherent in the utilization of clinical services directed toward *selected* clientele within the justice system. There are, indeed, psychologically-troubled offenders, in addition to those who develop impairments after their incrimination; both are in need of psychological assistance. However, as Vintner and Janowitz (1959) have pointed out, the presumption of client homogeneity is incongruent with our knowledge.

Finally, any statement may be questioned that begins with a clause such as "All offenders are . . . ." A model that sees all offenders as sick does not reflect the observed facts. It would seem that based on the present review, a selective-psychodynamics view most closely approximates reality and would, therefore, encourage valuable contributions of psychologists offering direct treatment services.

Situational Influences: The Use of Behavior Modification in Justice Agencies

Select two dozen college students on the basis of good personal adjustment, maturity, stability, and absence of criminality. Pay them $15 a day to participate in a simulated prison. Determine the roles of prisoners and of guards by the flip of a coin. And what will happen? There is a very good chance that you will find what Phillip Zimbardo did. In his experiment, this situation elicited from the participants every one of the behavior stereotypes of guards and of prisoners that appears in the Sunday supplements. Zimbardo (1971) writes:

> We had to close down our mock prison because what we saw was frightening. It was no longer apparent to most of the subjects (or to us) where reality ended and their roles began. The majority had indeed become prisoners or guards, no longer able to clearly differentiate between role-playing and self. There were dramatic changes in virtually every aspect of their behavior, thinking and feeling. In less than a week the experience of imprisonment undid (temporarily) a lifetime of learning; human values were suspended, self-concepts were challenged and the ugliest, most base, pathological side of human nature surfaced. We were horrified because we saw some boys (guards) treat others as if they were despicable animals, taking pleasure in cruelty, while other boys (prisoners) became servile, dehumanized robots who thought only of escape, of their own individual survival and of their mounting hatred for the guards.

While there are some major problems in accepting the Zimbardo study as a true analogue, the principle of behavior being molded extensively by the environment has a firm basis in the history of societal response to offenders. In the early days of United States corrections, the motivation for removing

70   offenders from the community was to provide for them a contemplative setting in which desirable change could occur through meditation and penitence. The Walnut Street Jail in Philadelphia, with its Quaker goals of self-reflection, is such an example. In the same manner, the current actions of the juvenile courts whereby adjudicated delinquents are removed from old settings, are based on the aspiration that life in a new setting may abort, or at least deter, future law-violations.

ENVIRONMENTAL MANIPULATION

The conception of situational influences as primary causal factors is not incorporated in the clinical model. While the clinical thesis is that most of the impetus for behavior lies within the client himself, adherents to the importance of situational and environmental factors suggest that the source of most behavior is external. This controversy in general theory (Lewin, 1935) has its resolution in the interaction of the two influences. Within the behavior modification framework, this resolution may be attained as the subject changes his reinforcement contingencies. In the examination of the behaviors of justice clients, strong evidence indicates that situational factors lend themselves equally well to study and intervention by behavioral scientists.

Street, Vintner, and Perrow (1966), interested in treatment factors which contributed to change in youthful offenders, found that outcome behavior was not predictable from personality variables descriptive of their clientele. Rather, they demonstrated that the philosophy, administrative goals, and organization of the correctional facilities were the major contributing factors.

APPLICATION OF BEHAVIOR MODIFICATION
IN THE JUSTICE SYSTEM

In a field where successes are so rare that they draw national attention, many of the justice agency achievements have resulted from the application of behavioral science knowledge. The Guided Group Interaction approach and therapeutic communities are two examples of ways in which clinical goals have been incorporated into justice agency operations. The Guided Group Interaction Settings at Highfields, Essexfields, Provo, and Pinehills have been discussed at length elsewhere, as have the therapeutic communities.

The major situational technology employed by behavioral scientists has been behavior modification through contingency controls and token economies (Cohen, Goldiamond, Filipczak & Pooley, 1968; Cohen & Filipczak, 1971). These techniques have been used in both community and institutional settings; they represent one of the burgeoning psychology methodologies applied to justice clients.

In a typical statement of position, Skinner (1953) remarks:

The practice of looking inside the organism for an explanation of behavior has tended to obscure the variables which are immediately available for a scientific analysis. These variables lie outside the organism, its immediate environment and in its immediate environmental history. They have a physical status to which the usual techniques of science are adapted, and they make it possible to explain behavior as other subjects are explained in science.

Similarly, Bandura (1969) indicates:

behaviors that may be detrimental to the individual or that depart widely from accepted social and ethical norms are considered not as manifestations of an under-lying pathology but as ways, which the person has learned, of coping with environmental and self-imposed demands.

There have been an increasing number of studies and demonstration projects using behavior modification procedures with offenders. Indeed behavior modification represents one of the newest and most wide spread psychological approaches being introduced into justice settings. Table 5 presents 12 such studies. In all of them, at least some of the target behaviors were modified in the desired directions. Some studies were made with samples of 1 or 2 subjects, in highly controlled environments, with limited target behaviors (Burchard & Tyler, 1965). At the other extreme, one study was made of an entire institution, which included 394 subjects participating in a token economy, using performance-contingent parole (DeRisi, 1971). In the modification of programmed educational output of prison inmates, the results have been uniformly positive. Other behavior changes in the studies include: a decrease in aggressive behaviors; a decrease in the use of hostile and aggressive statements; a reduction of destructive actions; a greater compliance with institutional rules; and an increase in in-program time.

Patterson, Cobb, and Ray's (1972) behavior modification procedures are particularly noteworthy. Their approach was to train parents of aggressive, disturbed children. The parents were instructed in the principles, in the language, and in some problem-solving applications of social learning theory. The results, in a series of studies using careful observation of the children, suggest that parents can quickly and inexpensively be trained in methods which reduce their children's deviant behaviors.

APPEAL OF THE BEHAVIOR MODIFICATION APPROACH

The popularity of such programs may be attributed to a number of causes:
1. There is a well-developed behavioral technology available in the area of social learning theory.
2. The existence of controlled settings for justice clients permits manipulation of external reinforcement variables.

TABLE 5

Behavior Modification with Offenders

Authors	Settings	Subjects
Burchard & Tyler (1965)		1 destructive youth who had not responded to other treatments.
Clements & McKee (1968)	Prison.	16 adult male inmates.
DeRisi (1971)	Institution for delinquent boys.	394 male wards of California Youth Authority.
Horton (1970)	Home for delinquent mentally-disturbed children	6 male delinquent youths.
Ingram, et al. (1970)	Institution for delinquent boys.	20 male delinquent youths.
McKee (1969)	Experimental center within Draper Prison.	Adult male inmates.
Patterson, Cobb, & Ray (1972)	Homes.	13 aggressive problem children.
Phillips, et al. (1971)	Community residential center and rehabilitation home.	15 male delinquent youths.
Schwitzgebel (1967)	Community street corners.	Male delinquent youths.
Tyler (1967)	Institution for delinquents.	1 male delinquent youth.
Tyler & Brown (1967)	Institution for delinquent boys.	Male delinquent youths.
Von Holden (1969)	U.S. Disciplinary Barracks.	Military prisoners.

Reinforcement	Target Behavior and Results
Tokens exchangeable for food and trips.	Destructive actions decreased in number and severity.
Money, contingency contracts, use of rest area facilities, and other items from a "reinforcement menu."	Number of frames completed daily in programmed instruction increased an average of 20% over baseline every week for four weeks.
Behavior change units (BCU's) and token economy scrip. (BCU's earn right to appear before parole board.) Use of weekly contingency contracts.	Behaviors which make it convenient for staff to operate institution (living routines; rule adherence; cooperation) improved. Academic performance improved. Behavioral deficiencies lessened and counseling was sought. 15 month follow-up yielded 35% recidivism vs. 50% recidivism for controls.
Beans which were exchanged for cash in card game of "War." Points (without exchange or material value) in game of "Steal the bacon."	Aggressive and non-aggressive behaviors in card game each increased when alternatively reinforced. Same pattern to lesser extent in "Steal the Bacon."
Novel activity, points, time-out.	Improved completion of training program (as opposed to punitive stay in segregation unit).
Points, certificates, contingency contracts.	Programmed-instruction output in language usage, interpersonal skills, and academic subjects all improved in several studies.
Time-out and other social learning techniques implemented by parents.	Targeted deviant child behaviors, e.g., hitting, whining, non-compliance, diminished 46% from baseline.
Points leading to entertainment, recreation privileges, and snacks.	Punctuality with respect to meals; cleanliness, monetary savings, and knowledge of current events all improved.
Money, food. Subjects were given "jobs" to talk into tape recorders.	Use of positive statements about others and punctuality with respect to work increased. Use of hostile comments, non-verbal tactlessness, not changed.
Sleeping on a mattress, wearing own clothes.	School performance greatly improved.
Subjects taken immediately to time-out room for misbehavior around the pool table.	General misbehavior decreased when time-out room used, and increased when verbal reprimands used.
Food, snacks, reading matter, release from disciplinary segregation.	Compliance with prison rules increased in segregation. 56% functioned successfully in 60-day follow-up. (Baseline rate was 44%)

74   3. To the public, the notion of behavior modification carries implication of doing something *to*, rather than *for*, the offenders. This may be highly acceptable to those who believe in a combination punitive and therapeutic approach.

4. The emphasis on reinforcing immediate, specific, and objective behaviors provides an acceptable philosophic, legal, and humanistic position. When this position is adhered to, the individual does not continue to be tried after conviction for his offense: he does not have to relive or in some way demonstrate a change in early childhood behaviors. Rather, the focus on current behavior permits an objective evaluation of observed change in immediate behavior.

The literature suggests that the manipulation of a number of environmental variables for justice clients is wide spread and is quite effective for specified goals. Indeed, adopting the process of carefully specifying behavioral goals represents an important, positive step for justice agencies. The issue, however, concerning the relationship of the externally controlled behaviors to free world functioning and to future law-abiding activities of the client, remains unresolved. Furthermore, there always remains the question of the right of the programmer or society to choose the behavior to be modified.

The behavior modification technology has been employed largely by itself. In one of the few differential treatment comparisons, a youth institution organized fully on behavior modification principles was compared to one organized and run on transactional analysis treatment principles (Jesness, 1970). Youth at both institutions showed positive gains beyond baseline expectations in grade level achievement, in Jesness Behavior Checklist improvement, and in reduction of time in detention. Of these measures, the greater reduction in the use of detention in the behavior modification school, was the only significant difference between the institutions. Little additional information is generally available about the comparative effectiveness of this, as opposed to other, procedures for changing the behavior of law violators. While the findings discussed here are positive, they do not rule out the contributions made by a variety of intrapsychic and transactional methodologies in dealing with offenders. They suggest an additional component in the treatment arsenal. An interesting attempt to "marry" the behavior modification approach with the more clinical viewpoint was made by Levinson, Ingram, and Azcarete (1968) when they combined group therapy with a behavior modification paradigm.

SUMMARY

No single model or approach characterizes all behavior modification programs in justice settings. There is variety in the theoretical underpinnings, in the methods of implementation, in the reward systems, and in the target behaviors. A comprehensive review of these issues may be found in *Behavior* *Modification and Corrections* by Bishop and Blanchard (1971).

The application of behavioral modification technology to the field of justice represents a basic academic contribution of psychology. Although not initially demanded by the justice agencies themselves, the proprietary interests and skills of psychologists were applied in justice settings. The utilization of behavior modification principles evolved from existing academic knowledge. Similarly, there are many other approaches within the areas of social, industrial and clinical psychology that lend themselves to such transplantation.

As has been the case with past treatment strategies which have waxed and waned in the justice firmament, behavior modification is viewed as *an* approach, rather than as *the* technology. Its practitioners continue to discover ingenious ways of effectively utilizing behavior modification principles within the justice system's treatment components. The question is not: is behavior modification good or bad? Rather, it is: under what circumstances, and to what ends is the behavior modification approach effective? There are no panaceas. A variety of treatment approaches must be utilized to selectively reach many in the broad spectrum of personality types who find their way into the justice system.

Special Applications to Corrections 8

With the full knowledge that the contents of all his locked files may and probably will be read by inmates that evening, the psychologist at a large midwestern prison waits for the 4 p.m. whistle so he may go home. Several routine things that have happened in his day are of interest to us. He received four pieces of mail: two letters from colleagues, one advertisement from a book publisher, and a newsletter from a professional organization. All had been opened in the prison mail room, stamped with the date of arrival, and sent to his office.

He administered a group test to 12 new prisoners, and interviewed 3 of them for the required initial psychodiagnostic evaluation. He dictated reports, of 200 words each, on 2 of last week's new arrivals. When they are typed by the inmate clerks, they will be sent "up front," read by the two deputy wardens, and placed in the prisoners' files. The reports will be read again when the inmate is assigned to a job and custody level. However, 95% of the inmates are assigned to medium custody, single cells, and to maintenance jobs. No information from the report is used in any actual decision-making.

Finally, during the day he had two prisoners scheduled for individual psychotherapy sessions. One was 15 minutes late and the other did not show up at all. When the psychologist inquired, it appeared that a pass had not been issued for the inmate that didn't arrive.

Miles away at Countryside Prison, the work day is ending for another

78   psychologist. He is hurrying to the disciplinary segregation unit to see if the experimental token economy and behavior modification program is understood by the new correctional officers on that incoming time shift. During the day, he has talked twice with the warden. First, on the telephone, they discussed a supervisor in the upholstery shop who seems to be growing overly suspicious and accusatory. Second, in a conference of department heads, they discussed the increasing numbers of young addicts arriving on Breaking and Entering convictions.

This psychologist conducts two psychotherapy groups every week and treats three individual clients. Today he had sessions with two of them; one of the prisoners was on time and the other was late. The correctional officer escorting the late prisoner to the psychologists' office explained that the delay was caused by the inmate having to complete a section of the test he was taking for his general equivalency high school diploma. The correctional officer knew the psychologist from the inservice and new-officer training program, in which the psychologist had been involved.

Before he leaves, the psychologist checks his schedule for the next day. He will be supervising the four volunteer counselors who are graduate students at the nearby university; he will meet with one of his psychotherapy groups; he will check on the screening evaluations done by his technicians to see if any prisoners have been identified who need to undergo a full assessment process; and he will be writing to some friends for help in filling the new position added for a psychologist. He is concerned about finding some time to assess the effectiveness of the pilot token-economy program, by analyzing the data he and a university consultant have collected.

The two prototypes described here reflect the observation that there is no single role model or level of satisfaction that is generally descriptive of psychologists in corrections. In different settings—and even in similar settings—psychologists function very differently.

This can be conceptualized as resulting from the differences in prisons, in the psychological personnel, or as a result of interactional processes. Our two case studies may simply represent differences in orientation of the psychologists themselves. In the examples, one is an isolated, often frustrated proponent of professional clinical services, while the other is an effective prison staff member. In the first case, the clinical psychologist is set up as a straw man. In the second, a major positive involvement in prison activities is portrayed.

The goals of some penal organizations are so intimately tied to, or based on, psychological theory that the functioning of their mental health staffs and behavioral scientists take on distinctive mandates. This represents an often desired, but infrequently achieved, pattern. Such organizational structures include the behavioral research prison and the mental health prison, as well as the specific problem-oriented strategies of these staff.

Before discussing examples of behavioral research prisons, some major ethical and procedural issues should be noted. These concern standards for research studies which are undertaken in total institutions, i.e., prisons, state hospitals, etc.

Prisoners or Guinea Pigs?

Images of experimental medical research at Dachau and Buchanwald may be conjured by the title "research prison." Indeed, accusations of such research have been made periodically toward some existing American correctional facilities.

The *Radical Therapist*, a psychological "underground" newspaper, wrote a bitter editorial attack in 1972 on the Vacaville, California State Medical Facility for prisoners. Vacaville was accused of imposing psychosurgery techniques on recalcitrant prisoners against their will; recalcitrance was defined in the article as resistant to political goals and behavioral conformity demanded by the staff. The Vacaville staff (Kim, 1972) reported that three prisoners had undergone brain surgery in the past, with voluntary consent. These prisoners were described as suffering from intractable temporal lobe epilepsy, which did not respond to medication and which included symptoms of recurrent violence. Such neurosurgical procedures were discussed between the staffs at Vacaville and a nearby university hospital so arrangements could be made to have such a neurosurgical option regularly available to the prisoners for treatment of temporal lobe epilepsy in the university hospital setting. The plan was dropped, in large part because of the negative publicity about it.

The issue of prisoners as research subjects has emerged as a controversial issue in other ways. It is not unusual for commercial companies as well as medical researchers to seek volunteers from prisoner populations. There is a substantial history of major breakthroughs in research based on prisoner subjects.

Two major problems emerge in this use of prisoner subjects. The issues are: first, the use of a project in the prison setting for manipulative purposes such as bribery or intimidation; and secondly, the question of whether or not a prisoner can *freely* volunteer to participate.

An example of the negative effects of research projects may be seen in the University of Pennsylvania study at the Philadelphia Holmesburg county prison. Davis (1971) discussed how this study of experimental toiletries and medicines led to concentrations of power and money in the hands of a few inmates, to forced homosexuality among the inmates, and to low morale, jealousy and favoritism among the correctional officers. The features in this particular study that led to problems, were the use of inmates as project em-

80 ployees and the relatively high pay for the potential disfigurement from project experiments. It is important to note that this represents an extreme in research intrusion on prisoners and prisons.

The second problem concerns the issue of the freedom to volunteer. In a penal setting with its omnipresent evaluation and control of the prisoners, "volunteerism" takes on a different meaning. In a free world situation it is highly unlikely that most prisoner volunteers would agree to participate in the same studies for the same rewards. The proposed Ethical Standards for Research of the American Psychological Association (1971) also raise this question. Principle 1.5142 states:

> When potential research subjects have such strong needs that they have little real freedom to reject incentives related to these needs, the psychologist may use these incentives to induce research participation only with the approval of an ethics advisory group.

In applications of psychological research to prisons, some of the same issues may be raised. However, they become much more diffuse and difficult to identify, since research and programming often meld into single entities.

The Research Prison

An occasional or even long-term investigation does not make a research prison. Many prison research efforts are the products of outside investigators seeking available human subject pools; such studies typically assume a transient and uncomfortable host-guest relationship. Similarly, studies resulting from the interest and the frame of reference of a single institutional staff member do not comprise a research prison.

A behavioral research prison may be defined as one with systematic and planned studies of variations in programs and of factors related to institutional objectives and theoretical issues. This definition carries with it the acceptance of the research mission in the organization and the use of relevant outcome criteria. In addition, possible information payoffs must be carefully weighed against manpower, time and costs involved.

The importance of the development of the research prison is the commitment it represents to a way of thinking about corrections. The developers do not believe in penal settings as essentially custodial centers. They identify as a goal, knowledge acquisition, usually accompanied by a dedication to the correctional treatment model. To some extent the behavioral research prison is being realized in several settings.

The Robert F. Kennedy Youth Center in Morgantown, West Virginia, is organized on the theoretical research findings of Herbert C. Quay (1972) and the programmatic studies of a number of researchers (Gerard, Quay, & Levinson, 1970). Staff and residents are grouped into living quarters and training assignments based on behavioral assessments and personality classifications. The educational program is organized around a contingency management approach.

An example of a portion of a prison devoted to behavioral research activities is the Draper Prison in Elmore, Alabama. Special living areas, contingency management of prisoners' behaviors, and manpower development programs, have emerged under the supervision of research and applied psychologists (Clements & McKee, 1968).

Within California corrections, an exemplary series of research programs have been based in penal institutions. From identification and treatment programming of offenders at different levels of interpersonal maturity (Warren, 1971), to the use of entire institutions for comparisons of behavior change techniques, there has been present a willingness to follow this concept of prisons as action-oriented behavioral research arenas.

THE MENTAL HEALTH PRISON

At what point does an institution cease being a penal facility and start becoming a mental health agency? The answer partly lies in the laws that govern the entry of clientele into that facility. The state of Maryland passed a Defective Delinquency Law in 1951 that created an unusual balance between mental health and penal objectives (Boslow, Rosenthal, Kandel, & Manne, 1961). Defective delinquents, defined as intellectually deficient or emotionally unbalanced persons who "clearly demonstrate an actual danger to society," are committed indefinitely until the deficiency or unbalance is relieved. The Patuxent Institution (a name selected deliberately without reference to hospital, clinic, or prison objectives) is the facility to which defective delinquents are committed.

The full acceptance and use of mental health treatment models for dealing with offenders makes this an important institution to examine. Its organization and staffing further implement the mental health model. Here the Director is a psychiatrist, and one of the Associate Directors is a psychologist. The ratio of mental health professionals to clients is about 1:11. For 400 defective delinquents there are 11 clinical psychologists, 8 psychiatrists and 14 psychiatric social workers. This agency has made an unequivocal manpower commitment to clinically treat the mental health needs of offenders. As prime treatment methods, Patuxent uses individual and group psychotherapy and a graded tier system.

Does Patuxent work? Hodges (1971) has conducted a three year longitudinal study of Patuxent releasees. The basic subject pool was a group of 1,340 persons who received diagnostic evaluations at Patuxent during an 18 month period. Of the 896 recommended by the Patuxent staff for commitment, 156 were not adjudicated by the courts as "defective delinquents" and, therefore, served as an untreated group. These individuals completed their sentences in the Maryland Department of Corrections. The partially treated

82 group consisted of 198 men who entered the Patuxent Treatment Program but were released against the advice of the Patuxent staff in court hearings. Of the 516 remaining men, 156 improved sufficiently to be awarded parole from Patuxent and 360 did not. The parolees were considered fully treated.

Recidivism was defined as post-release conviction, within three years, for any felony or misdemeanor. In the untreated group, 81% were recidivists; in the partially treated group, 71% were recidivists; and in the fully treated group, 37% were recidivists. Further, the fully treated group had a lower proportion of felonies and higher proportion of misdemeanors than the other subject groups.

Whether Hodges' findings significantly substantiate the treatment effectiveness of Patuxent is unclear, since many subjects in the confined group had not been paroled. It is possible that much of the high success rate results from good parole selection procedures and not from treatment.[6]

The prototype for full assimilation of mental health goals in institutions for socially deviant populations, is Maxwell Jones' work at the Industrial Neurosis Unit at Belmont Hospital in England. Jones (1953) changed the behavior patterns of persons who were evaluated as having severe character disorders and deemed not amenable to conventional treatment. He created an intensive cultural milieu unit, within which intensive relationships and shared responsibility existed for the residents' behaviors.

The transplantation of the therapeutic community concept into American penal settings has taken place with some apparent success in a number of places. Among these are: the Air Force's 3,320th Retraining Group in Denver, Colorado, which has organized the staff in its multidisciplinary therapeutic community into treatment teams, and reports restoration-to-duty success rates of over 80% (Broder, 1970); several U.S. Penitentiaries, such as those located at Marion, Illinois, and Milan, Michigan, in which segments of the institution have been set aside for use as therapeutic communities; and a number of intensive treatment units for drug- and alcohol-related offenders which have been developed in several state and federal correctional facilities.

H.M. Prison Grendon in England and the Institution for Psychopathic Criminals in Herstedvester, Denmark, both embody therapeutic community influences integrated with traditional psychiatric treatment (Sturup, 1969). The harmonious mobilization of staff and peer attitudes has been described as the key agent in the successes at Grendon and Herstedvester; however, the reports of success at Grendon have been variable (Parker, 1970). At

---

[6]If one were to assume that the institutionally retained group would recidivate at the same rate as the court-ordered releasees, then the estimate of the parole violation rate increases to about 60%. However, the goal of protecting society does seem to be met by continued incarceration of these retained inmates.

Herstedvester, castration was reported to be one of the most important and   83
successful treatment programs for sex offenders in the 1950's (Abrahamsen,
1960). In a more recent evaluation of Herstedvester, Morris and Hawkins
(1970) observe that for these extremely difficult offenders, the success rate
is about 50% for both initial and successive paroles. Thus after 10 years, 90%
of any entering group of these very dangerous, disturbed offenders are
living in their communities without committing serious law-violations.

MINIMUM STANDARDS FOR MENTAL HEALTH STAFFING

A standard is established to provide a measure of the quality, value or
extent of any project or service. Before Ralph Nader, *Consumer Reports* and
the rise of federal protective agencies, the determination of the quality of a
product was rather elusive. It was a personal judgment, supplemented by
considerable faith.

The delivery of quality professional services continues to be difficult to
assess. Among mental health related services, the ambiguity and subjectivity
are particularly great. The problem in evaluating the quality and quantity of
such services, as well as client needs for them, is due to several factors.
First, because basic adjustment problems are so widespread, a large portion of
the American population would seek mental health assistance if they could
compare themselves to a mental health ideal. Second, the pattern in establishing such services is that supply follows demand. No matter how great its
staff size, it is a rare clinic that does not have a waiting list. Third, with the
advent of community psychiatry and psychology, the definition of target
behaviors and clients becomes very broad and diffuse. Fourth, the staff-
patient treatment ratio is a direct function of the theory and treatment methodology of the practitioner. And last in this incomplete list, mental health
service responsibilities frequently are assumed, at least in some part, by
persons not identified as specialists in the field. These factors are all impediments to the articulation of minimum standards for mental health services in
justice agencies in general, and in correctional settings in particular.

The demand for specifying mental health staffing patterns arises from
at least two sources. The first is the budget and program planners. Every
year in justice agencies, administrators in charge of mental health services are
asked to identify the funds necessary for hiring mental health professionals,
and to determine what personnel are needed, and what changes in services or
programs are appropriate. Similarly, in planning for the staffing of new institutions or agencies, the same questions arise: How many? Of what kind? And
for what purposes?

The second source demanding psychology program standards, which has
recently emerged, is the judiciary. A landmark case was decided in Alabama in
1972. Federal District Judge Frank Johnson, Jr., ordered the Alabama

84   Department of Mental Health to comply with the mental health standards that represent an accepted minimum in the state mental hospitals and in the institutions for the retarded. A similar suit filed against the Alabama Department of Corrections has been heard, and a decision will be forthcoming. With the notion of the "right to treatment" (Bazelon, 1969) now widely debated and selectively implemented in mental hospital settings, the same principles in the form of a "right to rehabilitation" are clearly becoming substantial correctional concerns. This issue can be addressed by identifying minimum standards. However, such staffing patterns have to be preceded by the question: for what purpose?

Objectives

The setting of standards must be considered in the context of objectives and functions. One frequent approach is to simply specify that for so many clients there should be one psychologist, or psychiatrist, or social worker. Such standards tend to be arbitrary in character, unless clear objectives are specified. Even in such goal-defined cases, a degree of abritrariness remains.

Mental health objectives may be evaluated with respect to the extent that they contribute to the primary mission of the organization or to the primary needs of society. A trade-off decision is often made. That is, how much does fulfilling one part of the objectives, through the allocation of certain funds, limit some other aspect of the broader goals. In other words, one way to ascertain this is to ask the question: who gets vacation relief? The answer gives some indication of the importance of different personnel. In correctional settings, most often correctional officers have carefully scheduled vacation time. The mental health professionals are much less bound by concerns about maintaining continuous institutional services.

In answer to the general question of what standards for what purposes, a sampling of mental health service standards for corrections will be presented here, with a description of the accompanying tasks.

Task Force on Corrections
and the American Correctional Association

The Task Force on Corrections (1967) of the President's Commission on Law Enforcement and the Administration of Justice introduced its standards section with the observation that no single pattern could describe either average or minimum standards for the entire nation. Nevertheless, faced with the need to specify ratios and numbers, the Task Force did offer guidelines. It recommended for inmate counseling, that there be 4 counselors, 1 psychiatrist, 3 clinical psychologists and 3 caseworkers per 600 inmates. These are identical to the standards of the American Correctional Association.

A survey by the Task Force found that proportionately more correctional treatment personnel are in juvenile than in adult institutions. In juvenile institutions the ratio of treatment personnel (social workers, psychologists, psychiatrists and counselors) to inmates was 1:36, while in adult institutions it was 1:179. Further, it reported that there are enormous gaps between the number of treatment personnel employed and the number needed. There were 2,165 social workers employed and 1,803 more needed in all correctional institutions; there were 446 psychologists employed and 1,589 more needed; there were 234 psychiatrists employed and 659 more needed. The Task Force's Special Committee on standards did not deal with questions concerning allocation of duties, and goal-setting, for these 4,000 additional professionals.

Community Treatment Project

Since 1961, most of the boys and girls committed to the California Youth Authority have been randomly assigned to either a community treatment program or a correctional institution (Warren, 1970). A series of interviews lead to the classification of youths into general subgroups on the basis of level of interpersonal maturity. In a community center, counselors work intensively with youths in the community; counselor characteristics are carefully matched with appropriate client types. Follow-up studies, usually of 15 months, have indicated that this program reduces parole violation from one-third to one-half, compared to youths who follow the institutional route.

The caseload standard has been 12 youths per staff member. Although cost per youth is three to four times that of regular parole, the success and lowered expense compared to institutional care, has led to repeated program expansion and continuing development. The operating assumption is that low caseload by itself does not make the difference. It is only in this context, however, that treatment strategies can be followed and significant behavioral goals achieved. Thus, in a 15 month follow-up, Warren (1970) reports that clients who were well matched with project staff workers had a parole failure rate of 19%, while poorly matched cases had a failure rate of 43%.

RAPS:
Standards of the Federal Bureau of Prisons

Several years ago, the Federal Bureau of Prisons initiated a method of classifying inmates in order to allocate resources in a more rational way. Offenders were placed in categories according to a staff decision as to the inmate's likelihood of change. The basis for this judgment was subjective; the categories were Intensive, Selective, and Minimal treatment (ISM). Predictably, there was considerable variation in the decision-making process. An individual who was an *I* at one institution, might get transferred and be classified as an

86 *M* at his new institution. Further, there was strong evidence to suggest that after the classification process was instituted, there was very little differentiation in the way in which the three "types" of inmates were handled; i.e., programs might get filled with *M's* and there would be no room for the *I's*.

In January, 1970, a more objective method for determining treatment priorities was implemented. This system—which is known as RAPS (Levinson, 1972)—is based on both objective and subjective considerations in making the category determination: *R* stands for the subjective Rating which is made by the inmate's treatment team; *A* stands for the inmate's Age; *P* equals the number of Prior commitments; and *S* stands for the Sentence structure under which the offender was committed. For each factor, there are three or four ratings; e.g., for Age, below 21 is rated *1*, 21 to 45 years of age is rated *2*, and above 45 is rated *3*. Using this system, each inmate receives a four-digit code—one number for each of the four dimensions—and this code then places him into one of the three treatment priority categories, e.g., I, II, or III.

Category #I specifies that a great deal of time and effort should be directed toward meeting the needs of offenders so classified. The RAPS group #I has a staffing ratio of 1 psychologist or psychiatrist, per 100 inmates. In addition, there should be 4 correctional counselors, and 2 caseworkers. The progress of these clients is reviewed every 90 days at a maximum, and they are programmed in at least three treatment areas. They are never placed on waiting lists, and in other ways are considered priority clients.

RAPS #II inmates are the mid-category clients. Their minimum staffing ratio is set at 1 mental health worker per 300 clients; they are programmed in at least one treatment area and progress is reviewed every six months. RAPS #III inmates have the same staffing patterns per 600 clients. They are the lowest priority treatment group and are reviewed yearly.

This method is of interest because selected population targets are identified, and the criteria for placement in the category are objective, clear, and readily amenable to review and change. It is recognized that all inmates are not the same and that these differences should be acknowledged in the distribution of resources. One further aspect of the RAPS system is its monitoring effect. The requirement that progress be regularly reviewed on 10 effectiveness dimensions, according to a schedule fitted to the priorities, provides a lever for evaluation of programming and delivery of services to these clients. Further work is continuing in this area. A "second generation" computerized system for program monitoring is emerging.

Wisconsin Division of Corrections

One method of setting minimal mental health standards is to evaluate the existing services, assess the needs of the client population, and extrapolate

the necessary numbers of mental health personnel to provide needed services.
The Wisconsin Division of Corrections (Pacht, 1972) identified three kinds of
important clinical services: diagnosis, on-going therapy, and crisis intervention
contacts. The Division found that 36% of the institutionalized juvenile
female population, 33% of the institutionalized adult female population and
15-18% of the institutionalized adult males, received clinical services during
any given week. Several studies using well-defined behavior disruption categories (e.g., "disruptive users of alcohol" and "seriously impaired ability to
cope with their environment") have indicated that approximately one third
of the Wisconsin corrections clients need clinical intervention. In an interesting
presentation dealing with utilization of community resources instead of
Division resources, a ratio of about 1 psychiatrist or psychologist per 100
probationers in-need-of-clinical-intervention was proposed as one alternative,
but the recommended choice rejected the possible influx of professionals.
Instead, it was proposed to blend Division of Corrections services with the
development of potential professional and para-professional resources within
the local community. This alternative also has the appeal of not playing the
numbers game for staff-client ratios.

Should There Be Standards?

The objections to setting up staff-client ratios are very convincing, for
the arbitrariness in such judgments is undeniable. All too often such standards
are set without regard to actual needs or services.

Under circumstances which clearly specify professional achievement
goals, standards become a useful element in planning. It is possible that when
faced with the general question of how many psychologists and psychiatrists
are needed here, planners should automatically request information to determine the objectives, for which type of inmate, and within what kind of setting.
The numbers game becomes meaningful only in the context of goal-oriented,
specified activities for the professionals, and these activities, in turn, require
some consistent frame of reference. Mental health programming cannot be
separated from the total institutional setting. If there is no correctional program, there can be no mental health program. And if there is no identification
of treatment modalities and professional objectives, the development of
mental standards is a shallow table-game, with the budget planners doing
their functional equivalent of trying to avoid landing on "Broadway and Park
Place."

PSYCHOLOGICAL SERVICES WITHIN EXISTING
CORRECTIONAL FACILITIES

The following sections are drawn from material in the McGee-Bennett
report on needs for psychological services within the criminal justice system.

88 These services have potential application to detention and prison facilities and to programs that are directed at both adult and juvenile clients. While these possible services are subject to many limitations, including receptivity of the organization and availability of appropriate professional manpower, they indicate the scope and depth of psychological roles and contributions within existing correctional settings.

Consultation In Program Planning and Development

Correctional administrators often develop programs on the basis that they appear to be "good." Frequently, such programs are begun without taking into consideration their impact on the psychological functioning of both offenders and staff. The psychologist can be a valuable resource person in total program planning, development, and implementation.

One example of this is program planning to minimize negative impact. The psychologist can assist administrators by helping them understand how routine institutional procedures may result in negative influences upon some personalities, e.g., assigning individuals who crave stimulation to boring jobs in the laundry. At least psychologists can offer alternatives to a known dysfunctional procedure. They can conduct research on prison adjustment dynamics, and provide the whole correctional field with a better understanding of the effects of incarceration upon individual adjustment.

A similar contribution lies in developing psychological controls on disciplinary procedures. In both the juvenile and adult facilities there is a need for disciplinary procedures to help control inmates. The psychologist can often be a key figure in assuring that these measures are applied in a corrective, rather than a punitive or retributive manner. In addition, the presence of a psychologist gives the public some assurance that such controls will be present.

Quite often, administrators have promising ideas but need help in their implementation. The psychologist can aid the administrator in developing assessment methods to better anticipate how changes will be viewed both by staff and inmates. He can also help set up procedures to obtain program evaluation data.

Staff Training

Correctional staff need to appreciate the small proportion of offenders who suffer from emotional and personality problems. Further, staff need to have a special understanding of how to deal with acting-out behavior that does not stem from emotional disturbance. Such training may be directed at all staff members and focus on a variety of target behaviors.

The psychologist can function as coordinator of group counseling programs and continue in this training role. Even in the absence of such treatment efforts, spontaneous groups are an important part of the functioning of an institution; an awareness of group dynamics is most helpful.

Part of the responsibility accompanying such training lies in assisting staff/inmate interactions. In any situation where the key variable is "people relating to people" it is desirable to know one's own dynamics. Then, these factors can be taken into account in attempts to supervise or assist others. The psychologist can provide this kind of training in a variety of group settings.

Last in this category is the training of staff for a variety of treatment programs. Too often new and quite exciting programs are initiated and then somehow fail in operation. Unfortunately, they are often implemented by staff who carry with them obsolete attitudes and who utilize inadequate techniques. If new treatment programs are to be successful, there must be specialized training of the staff to carry out their new roles.

General Classification and Special Diagnostic Studies

Conceptualizing a large group of individuals as all alike, can result in dealing with superficialities as well as in distorting the positive contribution of available programs. Too often we see offenders simply "lumped" together. Individuals presenting unique behavioral problems may be housed together with people who are in the correctional facility for the first time. The psychologist can be of particular value in helping to determine how individuals can best be classified, housed and differentially treated.

Meaningful classification results in a description, or grouping of personality types, which assists staff in working with the inmate. Such classification helps staff gain a better understanding of the inmate's motivations. The psychologist can assist in identifying the program needs of inmates in the areas of vocational training, education, counseling, and psychotherapy. He may identify individuals needing special security housing, or those who represent unique escape risks, when these potentials are related to personality dynamics. He can suggest treatment strategies to more effectively address these and other problem areas.

Since the number of trained professional staff available will always be limited, psychological treatment may be reserved for those individuals identified as particularly in need of this intervention technique. Paid professional correctional counselors can be trained to effectively treat the less disturbed inmates.

The psychologist might provide information regarding inmates who need psychiatric management and supervision. A number of incarcerated individuals are suffering from severe emotional disturbances. The psychologist can effectively assist in the identification of those requiring this kind of specialized service.

Assessment of potential for violence is another realm of specialized assessment. Psychological diagnostic evaluations may aid in identifying those

90   individuals who have a strong potential for violent behavior; too often, however, the demand for accuracy is unrealistically high. The psychologist has no corner on crystal-ball reading—along with others, he can present his opinion concerning the individual's personality dynamics and how they might be related to violence in certain situations.

Within any institutional setting, there will be more than a few individuals presenting such unique problems that no one seems to know what to do. Often the psychologist can assist by providing a thorough diagnostic study and by helping the staff to understand some of the factors associated with the problem behavior. He may also be aware of other treatment approaches or be able to refer the inmate to other appropriate professional services.

Because of differing needs and limited resources, it is advantageous to determine the learning potential of inmates who are unable to read and write. The psychologist has skills and resources for determining intelligence levels.

While the determination of intelligence is an activity frequently demanded of psychologists in the correctional setting, there is little need for definitive assessment of intelligence except at the lower levels. Such evaluations can help staff to understand the level of capabilities of the individuals with whom they are dealing. Here, as elsewhere in the use of the psychologist in diagnostic tasks, the prime concern is to ask questions which will lead to some kind of differential programming. Speech, hearing, and certain kinds of organic brain dysfunction may be interfering with the individual's ability to learn. If these underlying conditions can be appropriately diagnosed, specialized educational techniques can be effectively applied.

Psychotherapy and Family and Marriage Counseling

Group and individual psychotherapy for selected cases is an important service. There are individuals within any institutional setting who can profit from psychotherapeutic intervention. Because many of the psychological intervention techniques were designed for middle-class, neurotic individuals, their wholesale application to all offender sub-groups may not be appropriate. Using research techniques, the psychologist can design programs for the appropriate utilization of psychotherapy in a correctional setting.

Family counseling is particularly important for at least some inmates and their families when one considers the long periods of separation resulting from incarceration. Often marital ties are not strong; the enforced separation is sometimes enough to weaken this tenuous relationship. The psychologist can provide valuable assistance to those prisoners and families that seek it, not only directly through family and marriage counseling, but indirectly in helping other staff to deal with these kinds of problems.

There is an assumption that individuals can be best "treated" within the social context to which they will return. Quite often the family or marital partner play a significant role in the individual's becoming involved in delinquent or unlawful behavior. Unless some effort is devoted to ameliorating these negative relationships, returning an inmate to an unchanged social environment will likely result in his failing to "make it" in the free world. Often such efforts can be initiated in an institutional setting and continued following return to the community.

Additional Services

Coordination of Community Health Resources.
It is unlikely that a sufficient number of mental health specialists will be available to provide all the direct services needed in correctional facilities. Available staff can arrange for and coordinate the activities of community mental health programs in their facilities. In addition, they can help channel the client toward appropriate community services following release.

Guide Outside Researchers.
Many people today want to help solve the problems of prisons. While some are naive social reformers and others are working in social policy areas outside correctional systems, there are those who wish to bring about change through a systematic study of present programs. The psychologist can be of considerable assistance to the prison administrator by helping such researchers shape their projects to deal with current problems of crucial significance.

Selection of Correctional Institution Employees.
The popular stereotype of the sadistic, brutal prison guard is no longer valid. However, individuals with personality problems that conflict with the appropriate supervision of inmates, continue to be attracted to this type of employment. The psychologist could be of considerable assistance to administration by providing preliminary screening techniques to insure that those with serious emotional problems would not be employed in this very important "people relating" occupation.

The selection of staff for special projects is part of this general task. Many efforts to develop innovative treatment programs have failed because they have not carefully identified the appropriate type of staff to function in the new program. The psychologist can play a vital role in assisting in staff selection for such efforts.

Development of Appropriate Space
in Correctional Facility Planning.
A social psychologist can make a unique contribution in helping designers of correctional facilities provide physical environments which relate positively to psychological adjustment. Psychologists involved in program development can work with architects to develop institutions in which the structures facilitate rather than hinder effective programming. Industrial and school psychologists can find relevant areas of employment in correctional settings.

SUMMARY

The varied roles that psychologists assume in correctional settings are a function of the organizational goals and milieu. The examples of behavioral research prisons and mental health prisons illustrate different professional objectives, expectations and activities. This matching process, between system needs and psychological services, was described for several areas in the McGee-Bennett lists. The question was raised of the minimum mental health staffing needs for correctional settings. The answer presented was that such decisions always have to be made in the context of the purposes of the agency and the specific professional role-demands.

Special Applications to Judiciary

In some ways, court work offers a more exciting challenge to the psychologist than any other role he takes up. Nowhere else are his findings exposed to such merciless criticism or his beliefs taxed to their utmost credulity. Moreover, his professional responsibilities are often greater than in any other type of professional work . . . [Haward, 1969].

The historical emergence of behavioral sciences in the judiciary has firm roots in the concepts of mental responsibility and competency in the English common law. As *mens rea*, or "intent" to commit the act, went through successive stages of definition and formalization, increasingly prominent roles were assigned to experts in the assessment of intent and mental status (Dreher, 1967; Sugarman, 1969). First medicine, then psychiatry, and fairly recently, psychology have been involved as disciplines of expertise.

It is from this background that a preponderance of interest has focused on the "not guilty by reason of insanity" defense and accompanying professional actions, testimony and postures. This chapter will not describe mental responsibility rules, testimony, and changes, for literature already exists in this field. Indeed, there probably have been more books and articles written on these topics in the past 20 years than there have been mental health practitioners regularly active in this field. Rather, the major issues will be described and some non-obvious roles and functions of psychologists will be considered.

Mental responsibility testimony focuses on the relationship of the

94 psychological examination findings to the five insanity "rules" (Allen, Ferster, & Rubin, 1968). If a hierarchy were constructed for these rules, it would probably range from the M'Naughten test at the conservative extreme to the Durham and Currens rules at the most liberal. In this context, liberal and conservative are defined in terms of inclusion of causes and personality factors. Some very persuasive arguments suggest that the differences between these rules are illusory, and are more readily observed in theory than in practice (Goldstein, 1967).

THE EXPERT WITNESS

Expert mental health witnesses have skills that reach well beyond the scope of the few criminal responsibility cases that are tried. They extend to areas of child custody, accident suits related to psychological functioning, and numerous other civil areas.

In a few jurisdictions psychologists are not accepted as expert witnesses; in some others they are accepted in spite of objections of opposing counsel. Their wider acceptance may be traced to the 1962 *Jenkins v. United States* decision of Judge David Bazelon in the U.S. Court of Appeals. In this case, the American Psychiatric Association and the American Psychological Association both filed *Amicus Curae* statements. The American Psychiatric Association opposed accepting psychologists as expert witnesses, stating:

> Psychiatry is the medical specialty concerned with illness that has chiefly mental symptoms. Clinical psychology "remains simply one of the possible methods" to be selected by the psychiatrist in evaluating and treating a specific mental illness [Allen, Ferster, & Rubin, 1968].

The American Psychological Association predictably supported the acceptance of psychologists as expert witnesses with a statement affirming their independent, scientific, and professional nature, training, and experience. Bazelon's ruling, permitting psychologists to serve as expert witnesses, observed:

> The lack of a medical degree, and the lesser degree of responsibility for patients which mental hospitals usually assign to psychologists, are not automatic disqualifications. . . . The crucial factor in respect to admissability is the actual experience of the witness and the probable probative value of his opinion [Allen, Ferster, & Rubin, 1968].

This new role has received mixed reactions within the profession. While the concept itself has been widely (but not unanimously) received with a "Westward, Ho!" expansionist enthusiasm, testifying on the witness stand has turned into a difficult situation in some cases. In particular, assuming advocacy roles and dealing with rigorous cross-examinations has been discomforting. It has been pointed out that a high degree of familiarity with courtroom and legal procedures is critical for a witness to be successful (Brodsky & Robey, 95 1972). Given such familiarity, there are still disciplinary and professional expectations that are not fulfilled on the witness stand.

There are approximately 50 U.S. psychologists who also hold law degrees.[7] Of these, Jay Ziskin has been one of the more influential and, perhaps, the most controversial. His book, *Coping with Psychiatric and Psychological Testimony* (1970), is a primer for the attorney seeking to negate such expert witnesses. The book is a collection of all the weaknesses and discrepancies in theories, research, and clinical mental health practice. This manual may well be an attorney's dream, but it is also an expert witness's nightmare. Certainly it provides a base of common challenge points, and may, for the uncertain witness, precipitate a bad experience.

The Experimental Psychologist and Actus Reus

Typically, attention has been directed toward *clinical* contributions in determining *mens rea*, or intent, of the defendant. However, the legal determination of the commission of the act itself, *actus reus*, has been facilitated by the development of analogue experiments on relevant psychological processes. The technique most often consists of identification of the key perceptual or motor process of the witness or defendant. This is followed by a controlled study leading to a probability estimate of the likelihood of the process occurring under similar conditions. Two cases reported by Haward (1969) illustrate this activity:

> The witness, a policy constable, noted the registration numbers of 4 motor cyclists who passed him in a town, just before lighting up time, alledgedly traveling at 60 m.p.h. Doubts concerning the validity of this feat of observation were raised by the defendant's solicitor, who asked for a psychological investigation. Police authorities gave 90 yards as the maximum reading distance of registration plates, the mean distance being 65 yards. Even with a 100 yards reading distance the exposure time of the 4 plates could only have been 3.5 seconds, and experiments carried out under similar conditions of time and light using 100 observers with 6/6 vision proved that only 5 of these could read correctly one of the 4 sets of numbers, and nobody succeeding in noting two, even after a concentrated period of 2 hours. The inference was, therefore, that the police constable had recorded the number plates at the scene of a road traffic accident in which the motor cyclists were involved a little later and some miles away from the alledged offense. The psychologist's evidence consisted of a brief description of the experiment, the result and the conclusions drawn. The police called in rebuttal a children's psychiatrist armed with a copy of Wright's Physiology, who testified that the eye could see moving images easier than stationary ones, and this was accepted as confirming the police officer's statement.

> A different type of perceptual problem occurred when two police officers, who had kept watch in a public lavatory, concealed in a broom cupboard for a week, arrested two men in flagrante delicto. One of the accused maintained that the

---

[7]This might be alternatively phrased as, "There are approximately 50 U.S. lawyers who also hold psychology degrees . . ."

policemen had mistaken the protruding end of his pink scarf for his penis. A reconstruction of the event as described by the defendant was photographed in situ, with variations in the position of the two figures. Using a latin square design, these were then shown to adults under varying conditions of light, exposure time and degree of expectancy on the part of the subject that the particular picture illustrated an indecent act. In 1440 exposures, 413 were perceived as illustrating mutual masturbation. In the particular phase of the experiment when the illumination and exposure time was closest to that obtained at the time of the alledged offense, one photograph in every 8 was perceived as portraying indecency. The case was dismissed, the 12% probability of error discovered by the psychologist [Haward, 1963] being considered reasonable doubt.

This study of witness credibility is performed in either of two ways:

> by showing the visual acuity, perceptual process or intellectual efficiency of the witness is such that the accuracy of the alleged facts are not beyond reasonable doubt, or by showing that environmental conditions obtained at the time were such that errors in observation were likely [Haward, 1969].

A related function is that of the *forensic actuary* (Haward, 1971). Published or specially constructed tables are used to estimate the likelihood of a sensory, motor or perceptual event. In one such case, Haward drew upon existing tables of light available one hour after sunset at the time and place in question, and disproved the possibility of a police officer's claimed observation. In more general applications Mode (1963) has reviewed six applications of probability laws and methods to the evaluation of legal evidence.

Psycholinguistics and Confessions

Arens and Meadow (1956) have reported on psycholinguistic analysis techniques in judging the authenticity of a confession. One of two defendants charged with burglary claimed that he was innocent and both claimed that they had signed prepared confessions after having been repeatedly threatened by the police. The police, in turn, testified that these were word-for-word statements of the accused. The confessions were analyzed on four dimensions: legalistic language, excessive detail, similar variations of answers, and sentence length. Comparisons were made with other language samples of the subjects and major differences were found. The two confessions were very similar in language, feelings and expressions. The testimony of the psychologist was that:

> upon the basis of his study of the two "confessions" and representative samples of the two defendant's written and oral verbalization, as well as the personality structure and psycholinguistic pattern, . . . the confession attributed to the defendant was not representative of his characteristic psycholinguistic pattern and that it showed evidence of fabrication or fraudulent alteration by outsiders [Arens & Meadow, 1956].

While the authors view this in the broad context of technology being mobilized in the protection of individuals from arbitrary government encroachment, it also represents a utilization of an area of psychological knowledge rarely applied in justice settings.

SIMULATION OF JUDICIAL PROCEDURES 97

The actors and their actions in courtroom scenes have become subjects of study by social and political scientists. While much of the information has arisen from informal observation and mixtures of discursive and baseline statistical reporting, a group of researchers are now applying controlled and rigorous methodologies. These behavioral science approaches typically are grouped under the general terms of jurimetrics, or the scientific study of legal problems, and experimental jurisprudence. These studies pervade every facet of judicial processes and draw on sociological, psychiatric, psychological, and economic research perspectives. For example, the collection of interdisciplinary studies by Simon (1968) included experimental studies of juror perceptions of expert witnesses, opinion change in juries during the course of trials, effects of plaintiff family status on court decisions, career patterns of lawyers, plea bargaining, and patterns of Supreme Court decisions. There is a whole genre of studies of simulated jury decision-making or of live juries in action. Representative of these is Padawer-Singer's (1970) research, in which judges' comments and newspaper accounts were selectively introduced to simulated juries, who were listening to tape recordings of real trial testimony and statements.

COURT—RELATED MENTAL HEALTH SERVICES

In almost every large American city, and many smaller ones, mental health clinics and services have been organized as part of the court administrative structure. Although the nature of these clinics and their staffing varies, there is overlapping of functions between clinics.

Pre-Trial Evaluations

Before one reaches the question of mental responsibility (one of the more "glamorous" courtroom issues) the question of the defendant's competency to be tried must be assessed. English common law holds that a defendant cannot be tried if he is not there—since, he cannot (under these circumstances) aid his counsel in his defense. In addition, in order to aid his counsel, the defendant must have an understanding of the nature of the alledged charges and courtroom procedures. These two issues, then, must be resolved *before* the trial can proceed. If an individual cannot be found competent under this test, then he (theoretically) "is not there" in the courtroom and, consequently, the trial must be suspended until such time as either the defendant regains his competency or the charges are otherwise resolved. Sardoff (1968) has suggested that the competency question applies even more broadly, including competency to consent to search and seizure and competency to make a voluntary confession.

98   Psychologists are beginning to play a more prominent role in the determination of competency to be tried—a function which had been almost exclusively in the domain of the psychiatrists. The use of specialized diagnostic facilities has led to more consistent, more specific and more objective competency evaluations (Robey, 1965; Cooke & Jackson, 1971).

Pre-Sentence Evaluations

As part of pre-sentence evaluations, many clients are referred for psychological diagnostic evaluations. Specific information is sought which would contribute to an appropriate recommendation to the court: probation or imprisonment. Carter and Wilkins (1970) have found that the psychological or psychiatric report is one of only five key decision factors actually used in the probation recommendation. The Federal statutes contain a number of special provisions under which a judge can request special study (psychiatric and psychological) reports to aid in establishing what type of sentence might be most appropriate in a specific case.

Problem-Oriented Services and Research

Some court mental health services are directed at developing continuing services and programs for groups of selected clients. An example of this process can be seen in the clinics offering services to sexual offenders and conducting research with these clients. While clinics in Philadelphia, Baltimore and Toronto have all organized specialized services, the Forensic Clinic of the Toronto Psychiatric Hospital has combined clinical, legal, and social problem research with direct services in an apparently successful operation (Mohr, 1962; Mohr, Turner, & Ball, 1962). The resultant information has yielded practical, as well as theoretical suggestions for dealing with pedophilias, exhibitionists, and other psychologically troubled sex offenders.

Family and Client Guidance

Both Juvenile and Family Courts have developed clinics which offer direct counseling, psychotherapy, and diagnostic services to justice clients. Referral to this type of agency is often accompanied by a diversion of the individual out of the adjudication proceedings. Thus, the practitioners of the behavioral sciences can have a significant impact on the judicial process, screening out those offenders who might attain greater benefit from alternatives to incarceration.

SERVICES PROPOSED BY McGEE AND BENNETT

The following functions are adopted from the McGee-Bennett proposals (see Introduction). They also fall under the general category of court-related mental health services, and point to optimal ways of utilizing psychologists and psychological services in court settings.

Assisting Judges in Understanding Relationships
Between Decisions, Processes and Outcome

Many judges have expressed the desire to know more precisely what has been the outcome of decisions they have made. Psychologists could make their research skills available for developing systems of feedback about subsequent adjustment, length of sentence as a deterrent, etc. Judges could thus come to understand what factors are associated with their decision making and how these decisions are, in turn, related to the subsequent adjustment of clients.

An area already suggested as having a potentially high return is the study of the judicial role and some of the complex psychological factors that play a part in the courtroom. While it may be some time before such investigations will be welcomed by all judges, the climate appears to warrant a beginning in this area. Study of the judicial process might include the evaluation of the probability of witnesses' perceptual errors, assessment of the veracity of those testifying, and inquiry into the psychological functioning of juries. In relating the behavioral sciences to the judiciary and the law, the results of such exploration could contribute to the continuing education of judges

Special Consultation to the Court

Functioning in the role of an *Amicus Curiae*, the psychologist could avail the court of his specialized knowledge, by interpreting the motivations and psychological functioning of the defendant, and/or acting as an interpreter of some of the more esoteric reports that may be submitted to the court. It may be that this role could be better fulfilled by a court appointed expert. To insure the rights of the accused, such experts should be used with the full knowledge of the defendant and his counsel, with an opportunity afforded for cross-examination and clarification.

Training and Consultation to Assist Probation Officers

At times a probation officer may feel that he is not quite "reaching" a particular client. Often consultation with a psychologist will provide guidance in handling the particular individual. The psychologist working with probation officers can suggest methods to limit setting, provide understanding in the methods of establishing relationships with clients who have difficulty with authority, work with the principles of group dynamics, establish effective half-way houses, and screen for appropriate vocational placement.

While many individuals quickly gain an understanding of the personality dynamics of their clients, they may be ineffective in applying corrective techniques. This often stems from a lack of awareness of their own possible contribution or a misunderstanding of the supervisory role. This can some-

100 times be corrected through an ongoing training program leading toward increased self-awareness.

Within almost any probation caseload, there are individuals who do not seem to respond to normal supervision. Further, outpatient community clinics may not be able to, or want to, handle offenders, for a variety of reasons. Therefore, special opportunities for psychotherapy should be provided within the probation framework. Probation officers can be trained and supervised in a wide variety of techniques, including behavior modification and relaxation methods in addition to the more traditional psychotherapy and counseling approaches. Psychologists are also in a position to solicit community help in improving service to probation and parole clients from mental health clinics, mental hospitals, and individual clinicians. The solicitations can range from basic "missionary work" (encouraging mental health people to open their doors and minds to the problems of correctional clients) to arranging assessment and treatment sessions for specific clients.

Provide Guidance in Establishing Classification Systems for Differential Supervision

The psychologist is in a particularly advantageous position to assist in differential supervision efforts. He can survey the literature, examine theoretical personality classifications, and develop a variety of supervision techniques to meet the needs of various groups of individuals. Sometimes it is much simpler to describe what a classification system should provide than it is to make it work. Again, the psychologist can make a contribution by developing clearly stated specifications for the establishment of specialized probation caseloads.

Provide Research Capability for the Evaluation of Probation Programs

The entire field of criminal justice suffers from a paucity of evaluation of current efforts. This is especially true in the area of probation. A variety of supervision techniques are being employed; these are selected, then expanded or eliminated on the basis of intuitive feelings as to whether they are "good" or ineffective. Appropriate study designs can be developed by psychologists which will provide administrators with some understanding as to which programs offer the greatest effectiveness for the costs involved.

SUMMARY

This overview of psychologists' functions and activities in the judicial areas of the justice system has indicated a variety of skills and settings in which they are applied. The emergence of the psychologist as an expert witness was seen as part of a broad developmental process, including the experimental replication of key factors in evidence, and the offering of clinical and research consultation to judges. It may be through these ex- panded and creative uses of professionally qualified personnel that behavioral scientists will be both better utilized and drawn into judicial functions.

CRIMINAL INVESTIGATION

I went on to explain my reasoning about the [Mad] Bomber's personal habits, his paranoiac avoidance of visible flaws. "He goes out of his way to seem perfectly proper, a regular man. He may attend church regularly. He wears no ornament, no jewelry, no flashy ties or clothes. He is quiet, polite, methodical, prompt. . . . Education: at least two years of high school. The letters seem to show that. They also suggest that he's foreign-born or living in some community of the foreign-born. . . . He is a Slav. . . . One more thing," I said, my eyes closed tight. "When you catch him—and I have no doubt you will—he'll be wearing a double-breasted suit." "Jesus!" one of the detectives whispered. "And it will be buttoned," I said.

On one of my visits [to Matteawan State Hospital], I had the Mad Bomber brought to the office I used. He was the picture of health; he was calm, smiling, and condescending. He was not wearing hospital garb as most patients did. Not George Metesky. He wore his double-breasted suit, and it was buttoned. In the Hospital, he was a model inmate, complied with all orders, went to church regularly . . . [Brussel, 1968].

These excerpts from the *Casebook of a Crime Psychiatrist* were taken from James Brussel's descriptions of the Mad Bomber who terrorized New York City. The first excerpt was a statement Brussel made during the height of the police investigation; the second was Brussel's observation of Metesky after he had been caught and hospitalized. Precision in this kind of clinical intuitive prediction is, of course, rare. Nonetheless, it represents one example of the growing impact of the behavioral scientist and the mental health professional on law enforcement. This trend is particularly evident in the field of criminal investigation.

A liaison between psychologists and law-enforcement agencies has evolved out of the illusion that the psychologist is capable of predicting all human behavior. Reiser (1972) notes that the police department psychologist "will find himself being consulted by detectives of homocide division in regard to a bizarre murder having obvious psychological underpinnings and a kind of logical meaning beneath the irrational surface appearances." Reiser recommends that the psychologist in this situation interpret unconscious motives as well as develop predictive profiles of individuals threatening to commit murder.

In the investigation of crime, one of the problems regularly encountered is the relative accuracy of eye-witness perception and recall. The familiar classroom scene of a staged fight or incident, where the students' subsequent perceptions of the event are widely divergent, has its counterpart in the everyday world of law enforcement. This "make-believe of evidence" has been discussed with respect to subjectivity and psychological process by Marshall (1966). He has observed that perceptual inaccuracies vary as a function of the sensory cues, of the impact of stress, of the influences of interpretative judgments, and of the viewer's estimation of the event's significance. Similarly, people almost always perceive more than they can report, because their recollection of a happening is selective and limited by both external and internal processes. To paraphrase Santayana, people believe what they see— the problem is they are better at believing than they are at seeing.

The police, of course, are not immune from these processes. For example, in one study policemen were shown photographs of scenes in which "criminal details" had been planted. The study determined that those policemen who made fewer criminal interpretations were rated by their chief as more capable than subjects who made more criminal interpretations (Verinis & Walker, 1970). This kind of investigation of interpretive discrepancies among law enforcement personnel promises to be a significant path for future psychological inquiry.

THE POLICE DEPARTMENT PSYCHOLOGIST

In many ways, a full-time, in-house psychologist is preferable to the part-time consultant, who has been the usual resource in the past . . . the in-house psychologist will get to know the organizational structure and dynamics much more intimately and pragmatically . . . relationships can be developed within the department which will enable him to be perceived and accepted in such a way that he can accomplish things the outsider consultant can't possibly do [Reiser, 1972].

It is clear that a case is developing for the psychologist to be a full-time, departmental employee if he is to be both accepted and effective in a police department. Many police distrust outside experts, not merely because they are outsiders, but because they have instilled in the police the fear, perhaps based on experience, of exploitation or criticism as a result of contact. Shellow (1971) observed: "Most outsiders, especially if they are lawyers or social scientists, are seen as hostilely contemptuous of police, since these are the groups from which most prestigious outside criticism comes." Shellow suggests that there are four options for the behavioral scientist. He may avoid all contact with the police; he may assume the role of critic; he may offer specialized technical assistance; or he may "attempt to crack the closed circle, to get inside where the day-to-day decisions are made [Shellow, 1971]."

The issue raised is how best to change the organizational system. Reiser and Shellow provide an unequivocal solution. As psychologists who have had full-time positions within law enforcement organizations, they see change from within as the single key lever. They attest that after credibility is established, through a number of procedures and levels of involvement, the influence of the behavioral scientist on administrators and their policy decisions becomes substantial.

Some critics conceive of this full-time commitment as representing a capitulation to, and indoctrination into, the organizational values and beliefs. Thus, Reiser's and Shellow's emphasis on the necessity to appreciate the patrolman's occupational experiences could be interpreted as a loss of distance and objectivity. However, objectivity is not the sole criterion of responsible participation. Furthermore, the critics themselves are equally vulnerable to the charge of subjectivity.

When the activities of police department psychologists are examined, several characteristics become apparent. The role of the in-house psychologist emerges as a distinct entity. The feelings of police departments are much more positive toward their own full-time psychologists than toward outside experts. And the psychologists themselves feel they have considerable effect upon agency policy decisions.

THE ETHICAL ISSUE

The utilization of psychological knowledge in the achievement of law enforcement agency goals, necessarily carries with it the potential abuse of this knowledge. Thus, Chief Justice Warren in the U.S. Supreme Court Miranda decision, viewed the mobilization of psychological pressures to elicit confessions as primarily employed "to subjugate the individual to the will of his examiner." The examiner's display of confidence in the defendant's guilt, the facade of fairness, and the use of interpersonal isolation and specific interrogation environments, were all cited by Warren as examples of the psychological ploys to which the individual is subjected and which violate his constitutional rights. The issue concerning the protection of the individual is

106   also relevant at the community level. Psychologists, directly or indirectly, may identify pre-delinquents or high risk offenders, so that some official intervention may take place. In such situations, the identification process, without proper safeguards, could lead to the inappropriate attribution of guilt or labels.

Since considerable psychological information relating to the identification of human behavior is available (and much of this may be applied to law enforcement), a critical question develops: to what extent are the behavioral scientists responsible, at both legal and humanistic levels, for monitoring and maintaining control over the use of their knowledge and techniques?

SELECTION OF LAW ENFORCEMENT PERSONNEL

The Task Force on the Police, in the President's Commission on Law Enforcement and the Administration of Justice (1967) reported that physical strength and aggressiveness continue, inappropriately, to be the primary standards for police selection in many jurisdictions. The Task Force stated: "There has been a failure to stress important characteristics which relate directly, to the ability of an officer to perform the police function well, namely, intelligence and emotional stability." Employing these positive selection goals which presuppose the elimination of biased and unstable applicants, was seen by the Task Force as being optimally attained through the use of both psychological tests and oral psychiatric interveiws.

Several reviews of police selection procedures have been published. Narrol and Levitt (1963) reported that all of the 55 large cities studied were using some kind of psychological test for screening purposes. A critical literature review by Smith (1971) indicated that retrospective studies of police personnel files have been unproductive, that longitudinal studies have been few and inadequate, and that personality trait studies have been "only marginally useful." One of the recurrent difficulties inherent in such studies stems from the variance in the criteria employed in judging good police performance. Blum (1964) and Smith (1971) have described the difficulties encountered in arriving at consensual standards for determining successful police performance and personality.

One review of literature and experiments examined findings on police personality by comparing the Minnesota Multiphasic Personality Inventory (MMPI) scores of 203 newly selected urban police and 100 control subjects (Gottesman, 1969). It was concluded that police applicants show a striking homogeneity, in terms of a "fake-desirable" pattern and essentially non-deviant clinical profiles, and that special police norms are needed. These results place considerable limitations on making interpretations of police MMPI's. Such caution also applies to other areas of psychological screening of police. For example, Mills (1968) has written about the problems presented

to the psychological evaluation team by the largest category of police candi-
date rejectees. The team joke—with some apparent underlying accuracy—is:
"If we *all* like him so well, then he can't be much good as a policeman."

POLICE AS COUNSELORS

In August, 1970, 125 chronic juvenile offenders in St. Louis were chosen
to participate in an intensive counseling program (Metropolitan Police
Department, St. Louis, Missouri, 1971). Forty of these teenage boys had
been arrested at least eight times; the other 85 had been the closest friends of
the highest recidivists, and virtually all of these also had records. Three teams,
each consisting of three counselors, were formed. The counselors were
drawn equally from the Police Department's Juvenile Division, from the
Juvenile Court, and from the City Recreation Department. The youths
received a minimum of 10 hours of counseling or supervision a week, in
which the peer group was used to redirect social norms and free time activities.

In a 14 month follow-up study, 12 of the subjects were found to
have been arrested for serious offenses. Seventy-four were neither arrested
nor issued curfew or truancy notices. Independent evaluations by a consulting
psychologist and sociologist indicated that delinquency proneness had been
reversed in at least 57 of the boys.

Although this program is significant in itself, its primary value lies in
exemplifying the use of behavioral science techniques and theory by the
police department. Like many other police programs (e.g., the Montgomery,
Alabama, Police School Relations Bureau), it fosters a close working relationship between police and behavioral scientists in non-enforcement police
functions.

TRAINING

Human Relations and Sensitivity Training

The recognition of the need to alter some police behaviors has led to
incorporating psychological and human relations training in many police training programs. In the New York City Training Curriculum for police recruits,
350 hours of the 910-hour program are devoted to instruction in interpersonal
relations (Wetteroth, 1971). This training has taken various forms in different
settings. Mills (1968) used small groups, structured "bull sessions," and the
"prisoners' dilemma" game in his training program. Newman and Steinberg
(1970) have had individual officers lead discussions on police-minority group
relationships. Siegel, Federman and Schultz (1963) have trained Philadelphia
police in community effectiveness. They prepared written descriptions of 10
critical police-community incidents which were then analyzed at three to four

levels of police involvement. These levels are initial entry, data evaluation, decision-making, and consummating the plan.

Human relations training methods developed by behavioral scientists frequently evolve out of specific techniques for trainee involvement. For example, as a way of coming to appreciate citizen perspectives, the Covina Field Experiment stationed police trainees in the community, and disguised them as high risk police clientele, such as skid-row bums or hippies (Ferguson, 1970). Films have been used in order to stimulate police-citizen encounters and attitudes (Rubin, 1970), and to promote emotional awareness and control (Danish & Brodsky, 1970).

An "exchange-of-images" model was employed in an extensive training program involving Houston police and citizens. One thousand citizens and 1,400 police participated in these six-week training sessions of three hours per week. Sikes and Cleveland (1968) initially had the police and community members meet separately, to list their self-images and their concepts of the other group. Then the groups were gradually brought together. Although no follow-up was made of actual behavior changes in the groups, attitudes toward training and toward each other did become more favorable.

Sensitivity training differs from other human relations training in that it provides the police with greater freedom, a less rigid structure, and a focus on the individual's immediate behavior. Sensitivity training is also unique in that its goals are not specifically job-centered. The behavioral scientists who conduct such groups seem far more enthusiastic about their potential than the police participants. However, there have been mixed appraisals in both circles. Some view sensitivity training as a key device for enhancing an officer's self-awareness and for promoting better relations with his community. On the other hand, some group leaders have deemed such training either valueless or actually harmful and problem-creating.

Family and Community Crisis Intervention

In 1967, the Psychological Center of the City College of New York and the New York City Police Department began a Police Family Crisis Training Project. Bard (1970) reported that 18 policemen were selected to be trained in what had been demonstrated to be the dangerous (to police) intervention in family quarrels and crises that threaten violence. The project utilized group leaders who were also experienced psychotherapists. Two psychologists who were formerly New York City policemen served as orientation resource staff for the leaders. The police participated in an intensive four week training program which included formal instruction combined with family crisis demonstrations by professional actors. The psychologists consulted with the police unit members, as individuals and as a group. The training provided by this project produced the following positive results: the absence of any injuries to the crisis unit members, fewer family assaults, and

many more repeat calls for police intervention in family disturbances
(Bard, 1970).

A program directed at crisis intervention in youth and community conflicts, as well as in family crises, has been conducted in Dayton, Ohio. In
training 40 patrolmen, Barocas (1971) provided a one-week ghetto live-in
experience and a "conflict intervention training laboratory," in conjunction
with focused video-tape feedback. Follow-up results are not yet available.

The effectiveness and impact of the Bard and Barocas demonstration
projects have yet to be determined. Both projects, however, did establish
environments and provide techniques whereby the police, in collaboration with
behavioral scientists, could deal with some substantial societal problems.

Training in Mental Health Principles

An understanding of an offender's personality dynamics and motivations
can be beneficial to law enforcement personnel. Given this understanding, it
would be possible to deal calmly with the offender during the arrest and
booking procedures.

Police frequently must confront extremely active drunks, persons under
the influence of drugs, battling marital partners, and seriously emotionally
disturbed individuals at moments of crisis. In addition, the police must take
into custody violent suspects, including those attempting to escape apprehension. The officer must be able to ascertain, in a general manner, the
nature of the upset and the best means to cope with the various kinds of disturbed individuals. Psychological training, including role playing, can supply
him with the tools and knowledge which may lead him to the necessary
understanding. This training should promote introspection, enabling the
officer to recognize and to handle his own emotional problems. He should
also be led to understand how his problems may interact with those of the
individuals with whom he deals.

The psychologist can assist the policeman by providing him with a
knowledge of the mental health resources available in a community, and of
the time and means to contact them. It is important to recognize the proper
time to refer a problem to the mental health field. If the individual officer
begins to feel that he is the psychologist, he may run into difficulties. His
training should provide him with an ability to distinguish between a problem
which requires referral to professional and psychological staff and one which
can be handled on a more routine basis. The role of the police officer should
remain the primary focus; his role should not be clouded by the psychologiz-
ing of all police-related contacts.

A direct application of these mental health principles has been fostered
by the Law Enforcement Study Center (LESC) at Washington University.
Under the direction of David J. Pittman, the LESC had conducted conferences and prepared brochures to provide "dependable, scientifically valid and

professionally oriented training and guidelines." As part of this venture, an excellent brochure on "Mental Illness and Law Enforcement" was developed to promote constructive encounters between the police and the mentally ill (Burger, 1970).

SUMMARY

In summarizing this information, it becomes apparent that the psychological activities with police departments or officers are not founded on any one particular strategy. There are many differing professional assumptions and techniques. At their best, they are received by the police as important and positive; at their worse, they are seen as sources of problems, and not as solutions to problems.

System Needs and New Applications of Psychology

11

The persistence of major problems in any setting calls for the use of expanded or new approaches. In the criminal justice system the difficulties have been severe, pervasive, and long-standing. Although a number of positive contributions have been made by behavioral scientists and mental health professionals, this chapter focuses on possible, new applications and roles. These roles are based on current knowledge and represent a realistically achievable set of extrapolations from ongoing practices.

AMELIORATION OF ACUTE DISTRESS IN CRIME VICTIMS

Fiscal compensation to crime victims in several states is an indication of societal awareness of the victim's plight. Currently, mental health personnel are developing roles in the treatment of crime victims and the immediate aftereffects of subjection to criminal attack or other victimization should be accorded proper attention in a comprehensive criminal justice program.

While there are widely varying thresholds of distress, a crime against a person usually results in some degree of discomfort. A psychologist, or other mental health professional, can often help the victim through a brief but timely contact. Even in cases where supportive counseling is not required, victims of emotionally-distressing crimes might be seen, at least briefly. The professional resources could include community mental health personnel and

112   those specialists working directly with courts or police departments.

Psychologists may also mitigate distress by training law enforcement officers to deal effectively with the crime victim. Such training could accompany instruction in the intervention techniques discussed in Chapter 10 in order to alleviate distress in crisis situations.

OUTPATIENT COUNSELING AND PSYCHOTHERAPY
FOR LAW ENFORCEMENT PERSONNEL

In today's society, there are strong resentments toward authority figures. As a result, some law enforcement personnel are under severe emotional stress. Although society demands "law and order," it also requires police to avoid any use of force that might not be absolutely necessary to carry out their normal duties. If communities are going to maintain a police force of the highest caliber and the greatest sensitivity, many law enforcement personnel will need emotional support (Sokol & Reiser, 1971). Psychologists can assist law enforcement personnel to function effectively in the criminal justice sphere by providing them with counseling, psychotherapy and opportunities for ventilation.

A longitudinal study of the role concepts of police officers (Sterling, 1972), supports this view. Sterling reports:

> The condition of alert preparedness for the eventuality of dealing with threatening criminal matter may influence the totality of the patrolman's role performance . . . many assignments which turn out to be calls for service may be considered by the officer as part of the continuing rehearsal for the real thing. In light of these considerations, it is unrealistic to lament the changes in personality needs which police experience seems to produce.

> Since there is an inherent conflict between emergent personality needs and role requirements, it should be recognized that occupational adjustment will be difficult for the individual to cope with. Hence, the services of a qualified counselor should be made available to experienced officers. Although one of the functions of the police supervisor may be to perform a "first-aid" counseling function, this does not obviate the need for a professional counseling psychologist. The effective police officer is a perishable commodity. Like any precious investment, he must be insulated and protected from harm. A formal counseling program can be considered as a form of preventive maintenance.

The psychologist can and should provide police with opportunities for counseling and psychotherapy on a regular basis, and referral services when necessary. In order to insure that the individual law enforcement officer has easy access to these psychological services, law enforcement systems might employ such personnel as full-time staff members. This would lessen the possibility of stigma being attached to an officer who feels he might need help. Easy accessibility could also abate peer pressures against going to a "head-shrinker." Even those officers who feel no immediate need would at least be informed as to what type of help is available. In addition, it might be helpful to provide a psychological debriefing after major incidents, riots, gun battles, etc. The aim would be to alleviate in the individual the possible reinforcement of feelings of bias, prejudice or hate.

The same needs are found in a number of other justice personnel. Individuals who work in correctional settings often experience difficulty adjusting to the authority granted them in their employment. As with law enforcement officers, responsibility and discretionary power increase as one goes down the chain of correctional command. Therefore, the need for inter-personally-effective correctional and police officers is substantial.

The issue of possible scapegoating should be raised here. That is, why pick police and correctional officers as the targets of major new counseling and consultation programs, and not identify judges, legislators, psychiatrists, landlords, or any of the other myriad groups who influence human welfare and decisions? All of these groups should have ready access to mental health services. Police and correctional officers are selected here because of their large numbers, impact, and discretionary powers.

A community mental health principles is reflected in the extention of services to the "gatekeepers." The impact of the mental health professional will be much broader when he directs his attention to the justice employees who are in continual contact with many clients, then when he offers mental health services directly to the general public.

CULTURAL-RACIAL TENSION REDUCTION PROGRAMS

One problem area consistently encountered in criminal justice activities is fear and unrest related to minority groups. Tension is evident in trans-actions between justice clients, between clients and personnel, and between groups of personnel. Programming should be explicitly directed toward the reduction of tension as well as toward the elimination of causes. In order to achieve these goals, emphasis should be placed on the establishment of research and demonstration programs.

The University of Oklahoma has developed a Human Relations graduate-level curriculum. Students are trained in the skills required to effectively intervene in situations which have potential for racial conflict. Perhaps more individuals so trained can be recruited into the Criminal Justice System.

Among the programs currently in effect, the most prominent are client self-help groups. In these cases, behavioral scientists have major roles in establishing the milieu that permits such developments, in offer-ing back-up resources, and in selecting and working with key figures in the programs. An example of this type of program is the Wisconsin Division of Corrections' cooperation with the Milwaukee Commandos, a Black militant organization. The militants are permitted and encouraged to work with Blacks in the care of the Division. Similarly, the Inner Voices, formerly of the District of Columbia Correctional Center in Lorton, Virginia, is a Black activist group, which is officially encouraged to work with Black justice clients.

A predictable item in any list of demands accompanying prison riots is the recruitment of minority group staff. Black, Puerto Rican, Chicano, and Indian justice clients find themselves enmeshed in organizations led and staffed largely by white Anglo-Saxons. While there already are recruitment programs for minority group members, such programs should be assigned high priority. Problems in the selection of qualified minority group members are receiving increased attention from psychologists and other behavioral scientists (Baehr, *et al.*, 1971). The educational apparatus in the behavioral sciences must be accelerated to produce sufficient numbers of qualified candidates. The presence of minority group staff does not solve all racial problems. However, given a commitment to change, the objectives may be more effectively implemented with appropriate minority group staff.

Similarly, in graduate education in psychology and other behavioral sciences, the effectiveness of minority group members will be best enhanced by programs which stress the relevance of racial-cultural issues. However, there is frequently a conflict between loyalty to one's subgroup and to agency responsibilities. It is suggested that special courses and academic emphases be directed toward minority group members and their roles in criminal justice systems, so that the minority staff members can have the perspective to be effective human relations specialists, programmers and investigators, without being overly bound by conflicts between agency roles and ethnic loyalties.

Tension may be reduced in two related ways. The first method involves cross-cultural training. Both staff and justice clients are given a variety of experiences which lead them to an understanding of the lives and perceptions of other groups with whom they have contact. The second focuses on the actual interaction patterns between staff and clients. This would serve to increase the members' understanding of their actual transactions and to reduce the stereotypic thinking that accompanies tense racial-cultural atmospheres.

RIOT PREVENTION

Following almost every series of large city civil disorders and almost every major prison riot, a distinguished commission examines the events and submits recommendations to prevent reoccurence. One important contribution which behavioral scientists can make is to examine the existing scientific information in these reports and to work toward preventing such disorders. For example, it has been found that potential disorders within penal settings may be aborted by good communication channels. Communication and prevention processes include the means for grievances to be redressed, the participation by residents in decisions that affect their welfare, and the use of knowledge of group dynamics for positive problem-solving. Promoting a sense of community also serves to advance this objective.

Environments such as crowded living quarters dehumanize their residents and are related to prison disorders. Skelton (1969), in his study of a prison riot, has emphasized the function of physical setting in shaping the prisoner's behavior. In this respect, the behavioral scientist may be able to make a contribution in the planning and design of new physical facilities for justice agencies. One step toward mating architecture, criminal justice needs, and behavioral sciences was taken in an examination of correctional architecture. Sommer (1971) specified 27 proposals for design changes in penal systems. These proposals ranged from bland to ingenious. One example of the latter type, well grounded in psychological knowledge, was:

> Each inmate should be given control over the level of sensory stimulation within his own living space. This includes control of lighting and media, as well as the amount and kind of furnishings within the space [Sommer, 1971].

Such integrations of knowledge and needs might beneficially be applied to every physical structure within justice settings.

OTHER NEW APPLICATIONS

Prevention of Individual Violence

Some applications of psychology aimed at the prevention of individual violence, have grown out of the laboratory and the clinic. The work of Megargee (1971) has pointed to the existence of "overcontrolled hostility" patterns, in which serious crimes against persons are committed by individuals who show no obvious signs of hostility. Singer (1971) has identified in the mass media selected presentations of aggression (e.g., justified aggression) that seem to lower inhibitions against aggression. These research findings have applications in the early identification of likely aggressors, and in the policy issues of the mass media.

Many violence-prone persons seek aid in restraining their own violence. A few existing professional services, such as the Seattle Crisis Clinic, include provisions for helping the violence-prone. The number of such services, however, is small; more are needed. Their methods should be studied and refined.

In a related area, police have been shown to manifest widely varying propensities for enacting and eliciting violence (Toch, 1969). The classification, identification, and prevention of such iatrogenic aggression and physical hostility is another high priority application of psychology.

Products of the System

As new career roles are assumed by former offenders, the behavioral scientist has many opportunities for involvement. In selecting and counseling offenders likely to enter this employment field, in training, and in extending back-up services, the psychologist may increase the use of offenders as resources.

Program Evaluation

There are large numbers of justice agency projects and programs which have never been critically or objectively evaluated. This is particularly true of many small, local or regional projects. Behavioral scientists can make an important contribution by establishing an organizational structure, and by providing expertise that would aid in the evaluation of some of these projects. Furthermore, it is important for the psychologist to have sufficient input into the appropriation of fiscal funds to insure that substantial numbers of projects do lend themselves to evaluation.

SUMMARY

The issues of psychological aid for victims, of effectiveness and adjustment of justice personnel, of minority group problems, and of riots and disorders, are all serious and wide-spread. One of the temptations in writing this list was to propose a long series of far-fetched ideas that began with, "Hey, why don't we . . . ?" Instead, the proposals discussed in this chapter suggest applications which exist or are readily achievable. These proposals, if they are to be realized, require a major commitment by both psychology and justice agencies.

Graduate Education

Charles D. Speilberger, Edwin I. Megargee and
Gilbert L. Ingram

It is hardly necessary to document the concerns of American society with problems of crime, delinquency, and corrections. One need only peruse the headlines of the daily paper or the feature stories in the weekly news magazines to be convinced that crime and violence are among the most serious problems that we currently perceive. Law and order has become a major national political issue, and the events at Attica rank along with My Lai as a national tragedy which pricks the American social conscience.

If psychology is to have a meaningful role in the areas of crime, delinquency and corrections, it must develop educational programs that turn out competent professionals who understand these areas and have the requisite skills to make effective contributions. However, the development of relevant training programs requires a clear definition of the problems, a thorough understanding of the present roles and functions of psychologists in the criminal justice system, and of the needs of the system from the viewpoint of the government agencies established to deal with these problems. What are the potential contributions of psychology to the policeman, the judge, correctional personnel, parole and probation officers, and the various agencies with responsibilities in the prevention of crime and the rehabilitation of offenders?

We will approach the problem of graduate education in the fields of crime, delinquency, and corrections by first attempting to clarify the nature and scope of the general problem and surveying a number of relevant training

118 programs that are already in operation. We will then suggest several training models that might be appropriate in these fields. Finally, we will describe, in some detail, our own efforts at Florida State University (FSU) over the past five years in the development of a training program related to crime, delinquency and corrections.

THE GENERAL PROBLEM

Crime and violence are costly and widespread in American life. In response to this threat to society Congress has reacted by passing the "Safe Streets Act," to provide needed funds to search for the causes of anti-social behavior. These funds will help to provide laboratories for training research specialists in crime and delinquency, and for developing sophisticated diagnosis and treatment facilities supported by broadly based community programs aimed at the prevention and amelioration of the forces that spawn anti-social behavior.

A better understanding of the problems of crime and delinquency will require a great deal of fundamental research by psychologists and other social scientists. Since poverty and racial tension are important determinants of crime and delinquency, the needed research must be carried out within a broad framework with perspective based upon an understanding of the social and economic problems that plague American society.

Understanding crime and delinquency will also require a comprehension of the impact on the American character structure of the fundamental changes that are taking place within our society. Alan Harrington, writing on the subject of psychopathy in the December, 1971, issue of *Playboy*, advances the interesting thesis that our society may have come to the hour of the advent of "psychopathic man." According to Harrington:

> In search of justice, we find psychopathy on all sides, including that of law and order. For example, what fairness could Manson expect when he heard the Judge scheduled to try his case had attended a skit performed by members of the Bar—based on the hilarious perceptions of Manson's commune—entitled "The Family That Slays Together, Stays Together"?

> It is not so much that individuals who may be diagnosed at least as part psychopaths have risen to eminence and leadership in our country (there is nothing particularly new in this idea), but that the psychopathic ideal of acting out all desires has become routinely accepted, possibly supreme—even among people who are not psychopaths.

We have quoted at length from Harrington, not because we place much credence in his views, but because we feel that understanding crime and delinquency requires comprehending the basic value system of our society. These values lead to the diagnosis of a particular individual as "sick" or "criminal" and they determine whether that person will receive treatment or punishment.

Given the history of psychology, and its traditional expertise in psychodiagnosis and research, it is apparent that psychologists have several distinct contributions to make: (a) research is required to clarify the personality variables which influence deviant behavior, and in developing needed assessment instruments; (b) providing psychological evaluations of offenders that give sufficiently detailed information for planning treatment and rehabilitation programs; plus (c) staff training and consultation.

In the past, the efforts of psychologists in the fields of crime and delinquency have centered around prisons and correctional institutions. A clearly discernible trend, however, is the growing conviction in the field of corrections that the rehabilitation of offenders should be community-based. The President's Task Force on Prisoner Rehabilitation concludes that offenders should be diverted from imprisonment if this can be done with safeguards for society, and recognizes that many more community facilities and programs will be required than are currently available. To meet this need, the Task Force in its final report specifically recommended that:

> The Federal government should grant funds to the states and localities for the training and employment of substantially greater numbers of qualified probation and parole workers, both professional and paraprofessional.
>
> The Federal government should establish regional training programs to provide continuing in-service training for probation, parole, and all other correctional officers.

To summarize, it is in the areas of research and evaluation that psychology has perhaps the most distinct contribution to make to the fields of crime, delinquency, and corrections. It also has important contributions to make in consultation, in formulating and carrying out treatment and rehabilitation plans, and especially in training paraprofessionals in these areas. However, other disciplines such as psychiatry, social work, and educational and rehabilitation counseling, must share these responsibilities. As the focus of professional effort in the fields of crime, delinquency and corrections shifts from apprehension and punishment to prevention and rehabilitation, more effort will be directed to working in community settings. Psychological consultation, social systems analysis, and community psychology will become essential elements in graduate educational programs for psychologists who work in these fields.

PSYCHOLOGY TRAINING PROGRAMS IN
CRIME, DELINQUENCY AND CORRECTIONS

On the basis of the responses to an "informal" survey, we conclude there is considerable interest being generated among psychologists in the

120   fields of crime, delinquency, and corrections, but that, with a few notable
exceptions, there has been relatively little progress in developing training programs in these areas.[8] In an unpublished study designed to determine course
offerings in psychology relevant to crime and delinquency, Brodsky and
Heisler (1971) reviewed the catalogues of American universities. They identified only 14 courses relating to crime and corrections offered by psychology departments at 11 different universities. These academic settings and the
courses offered were:

1. Adelphi University: *Forensic Psychology and Ethics*
2. Michigan State University: *Legal and Criminal Psychology*
3. Middle Tennessee State University: *Practicum of Law Enforcement; Psychology of Criminal Behavior; Correctional Psychology*
4. North Dakota State University: *Juvenile Delinquency*
5. Ohio State University: *Delinquent Children*
6. Sacramento State College: *Psychology in Law Enforcement*
7. St. John's University: *Psychology of Delinquent Behavior*
8. University of Colorado: *Social Psychology of Deviant Behavior*
9. University of Kentucky: *Psychology of the Criminal*
10. University of Southern California: *Psychological Aspects of Crime*
11. University of Tennessee: *Psychology of Crime; Forensic Psychology*

This absence of formal courses within psychology is misleading. Psychologists have other types of training relationships with justice systems personnel.
Many psychologists are working informally with law enforcement and correctional agencies, and providing training in interdisciplinary programs
housed in other academic departments. A brief description of several of these
programs is offered to illustrate the nature of the current training programs
in which psychologists are contributing to training in the fields of crime,
delinquency and corrections.

Academic Correctional Psychology Training

The University of Alabama was recently awarded a substantial grant
from the Law Enforcement Assistance Administration of the U.S. Department
of Justice to train correctional psychologists at the BS, MA, and PhD levels.
These programs are directed by Dr. Raymond Fowler and include existing
courses in psychology, sociology, social work, law, and other disciplines. In

---

[8]In undertaking this assignment of discussing graduate education in psychology
related to the fields of crime, delinquency, and corrections, we initially considered conducting a survey of existing programs, and sought consultation from Stanley Brodsky,
past President of the American Association of Correctional Psychologists, and Saleem
Shah, Chief of the Center for Studies of Crime and Delinquency of the National
Institute of Mental Health. From them we obtained the names of a number of
psychologists whom we have subsequently consulted regarding what is going on in the
field. We are especially grateful to those who responded with detailed comments
describing their programs.

addition, there are specialized courses and seminars designed for the correctional area, and a range of practicum experiences which involve extensive
contacts with offenders, law enforcement agencies, juvenile delinquency prevention programs and community agencies. In announcing the initial grant for
the Correctional Psychology Center at the University of Alabama, Jerris
Leonard (1971), Chief LEAA administrator, was quoted as follows:

> The idea of this thing is to get more psychologists trained to work directly with
> inmates. We've got to do something to keep pace with the demands of our time. . . .
> We're trying to get to the individual prisoners and give some hope to them;
> prisons should not be a dead-end for people in trouble but should serve in the
> same capacity as a mental hospital; that is, to give some rehabilitation.

At Middle Tennessee State University, Dr. Frank Lee directs an MA
program in psychology which offers a specialization in correctional psychology. Students in this program take the usual core courses. There are also
courses on the "Psychology of Criminal Behavior" and on "Correctional
Psychology," as well as practicum training that involves field placements in a
variety of correctional settings. The program works in liaison with the University's Center for the Study of Crime, Law Enforcement, and Corrections, which provides psychological services and consultation to law enforcement agencies, the juvenile courts, and to the Tennessee Department of
Corrections. This program was initiated in September, 1970.

The Department of Psychology at Southern Illinois University has a set
of options in correctional psychology that graduate students may select. The
program, which is directed by Dr. Stanley Brodsky, does not represent a
formal subspecialty, but provides a "crime and corrections minor." Interested
students take a number of courses and practicum experiences which are
coordinated with the University's Center for the Study of Crime, Delinquency,
and Corrections.

Table 6 presents a comparison of the Alabama, Middle Tennessee State,
and Southern Illinois University programs, as well as the Florida State
University program, which is discussed in detail later. The communalities
include a strong emphasis on field experience and a synthesis with existing
graduate programs. The divergencies include the levels of the programs'
terminal degrees and the sources of field experience. These "In-House"
programs only represent part of the range of psychological-criminological
teaching activities, however.

Many psychology departments have training liaisons with justice agencies as part of ongoing programs in broad areas of psychology. Clinical psychology graduate students at The University of Hawaii, West Virginia
University, Eastern Michigan University and the University of Montana all
have the opportunity for supervised experiences at nearby correctional
agencies. In the Stanford, Buffalo and Texas graduate programs, students
from social and community psychology programs are active with offender

Chapter 12

TABLE 6
Graduate Education Programs in Correctional Psychology

	Florida State University	University of Alabama
Level	PhD	BA, MA, PhD
Thesis or dissertation	Yes	No (BA), No (MA), Yes (PhD)
Title	Clinical Psychology, Correctional Psychology subspecialty	Correctional Psychology
Field experience	Primarily Federal Correctional Institution, Tallahassee	Local and Area Correctional and Law Enforcement Agencies
Internship	Yes; but not at justice agency	Yes; but within justice agency
No. of students	12	20 (BA), 9 (MA), 2 (PhD)
Support source	USPHS, NIMH	LEAA
Support level/ 12 months	$2,400-$3,600	$1,000 (BA) $3,600 (MA) $4,800 (PhD)
Relationships with other departments	Up to 12 hours taken in Department of Criminology and Corrections	Offered through Center for Correctional Psychology
Academic notes	Required 3rd year critical review paper; summer clerkship; 5th year spent with Behavior Research Laboratory at FCI.	Non-thesis master's degree restricts entering into PhD program for 2 years.

Southern Illinois University	Middle Tennessee State University
PhD	MA
Yes	Yes
Clinical or Counseling Psychology, Crime and Corrections Minor	Correctional Psychology option
Vienna and Marion, Illinois, prisons	Tennessee Juvenile and Adult Correctional Facilities; Some Court and Probation-Parole settings
Yes; justice agency is optional	Not applicable
10	25
USPHS, State of Illinois	LEAA and Tennessee Department of Corrections
$2,400-$3,600	$3,250
Minor offered through liaison with Center for the Study of Crime, Delinquency, and Corrections	Half of students supported by Center for the Study of Crime, Law Enforcement and Corrections
Students often work as graduate assistants in Center for the Study of Crime, Delinquency and Corrections.	Strong background in diagnostic skills is emphasized.

124   populations.

There are also internships in applied psychology offered in justice agencies. The Monmouth County, New Jersey, Child Guidance Clinic works with ex-offender groups, acting-out juveniles, and correctional populations. The Federal Bureau of Prisons and the Wisconsin Division of Corrections provide internship training for clinical psychology graduate students.

The Johns Hopkins University initiated an internship in Public Psychology in summer, 1972. Intended for students in social, community or clinical psychology, the internship has 14 available placements. These include court agencies, state and local law enforcement departments, the offices of the Mayor of Baltimore and the Governor of Maryland, schools, an architectural firm, a housing department, and a traffic and transit department. Looking at the academic and internship efforts as a whole, it appears that it is not necessary to have a formal program in psychology and justice to involve psychologists in justice agency activities.

A number of psychologists who responded to our informal survey reported that their primary teaching responsibilities were in departments of sociology, or in interdisciplinary programs that cut across the traditional academic boundaries. Among these individuals, there seems to be a strong consensus regarding the importance of social psychology and inputs from other social science disciplines for those interested in the areas of crime and delinquency. The need to develop a high degree of sophistication in quantitative methods and research methodology is also essential for those wishing to do research in these areas.

It is interesting to note that there may be imminent jurisdictional disputes brewing between psychology departments interested in developing programs in crime and delinquency, sociologists who have been working in these fields for considerable periods of time, and schools of criminology which are often dominated by sociologists and psychiatrists. The development of graduate training programs in crime, delinquency, and corrections for psychologists should certainly attempt to work closely with programs that already exist and to develop a meaningful professional relationship with other disciplines.

TRAINING MODELS FOR PSYCHOLOGY PROGRAMS IN CRIME, DELINQUENCY, AND CORRECTIONS

The present circumstances that have served to stimulate the development of training programs in the psychology of crime, delinquency and corrections are analogous in a number of ways with the press of events that stimulated the development of clinical psychology after World War II. At that time, there was an unprecedented demand for persons with professional training in the mental health fields. Few formal training programs in clinical psychology existed. There was wide variability with regard to definitions of the field and convictions regarding the optimal content of educational programs that would turn out competent professionals. This set of circumstances stimulated the development of the first national conference on training in psychology, held in Boulder, Colorado, in August of 1949. This conference was sponsored by the American Psychological Association on impetus provided by requests from the Veterans Administration and the Public Health Service for APA to identify universities with adequate training programs in clinical psychology and to establish a set of standards and procedures for accrediting these programs. The 72 participants in the Boulder conference, who came primarily from academic institutions, identified, considered, and attempted to arrive at positions with regard to 15 major issues (Raimey, 1950):

1. Social needs and clinical psychology.
2. Professional training in light of a changing science and society.
3. Kinds and level of training.
4. Professional ethics and problems of training.
5. Background preparation for clinical psychology.
6. Core curriculum in clinical psychology.
7. Training for research.
8. Training for psychotherapy.
9. Field training.
10. Selection and evaluation of students.
11. Staff training.
12. Relations with other professions.
13. Relations with governmental agencies.
14. Accreditation of training universities.
15. Licensing and certification.

A "scientist-professional" model for doctoral training in clinical psychology was adopted at the Boulder conference. This model specified that training for doctoral students in clinical psychology would consist of a broad foundation in the traditional areas of psychology, such as learning, perception, personality, physiological and social psychology. In addition to training in basic psychology and in statistics and quantitative methods, students in clinical psychology would receive intensive training in the development of professional skills in psychodiagnosis and psychotherapy. The scientist-professional model was subsequently reaffirmed in a series of APA-NIMH sponsored national conferences on "Psychology and Mental Health" (Strother, 1956) and on the "Professional Preparation of Clinical Psychologists (Hoch, Ross, & Winder, 1966)." The reports of the proceedings and conclusions of each of these conferences have been published by the APA, and many of the points that have been carefully reviewed and considered in other areas of psychology are certainly germaine to the development of psychology training

126   programs in crime, delinquency and corrections.

It is obviously not possible to formulate conclusions at this point in time with regard to the kinds of training programs that should be developed in the psychology of crime, delinquency and corrections. This will require a careful appraisal of what psychologists are presently doing in these areas and a clear conception of the needs of the law enforcement agencies, the courts, and other elements of the criminal justice system for psychological services. Furthermore, there should be a diversity of training models, and considerable flexibility in their development, taking advantage of the unique interest and resources found in the training program settings.

Given the large number of issues that are relevant to the development of graduate education programs in crime, delinquency and corrections, it is important to focus upon those issues that should be given initial priority. The present report can only be a beginning. Before identifying the three major issues on which we will recommend discussion, we suggest that a start be made immediately to set up a conference devoted entirely to graduate education in crime, delinquency and corrections, to be held two years hence. The three major issues on which we feel clarification is required at the outset are: (a) Level of training. (b) Locus of training. (c) Relation of the training program in crime, delinquency, and corrections to other graduate programs in psychology, and related social science disciplines.

Level of Training

The need for professional personnel in the fields under consideration has already generated training programs at the BS, MA, and PhD levels. It is recognized that the manpower needs in the field can never be adequately met with doctoral level personnel. After more than two decades of heavy financial support for doctoral programs in clinical psychology, less than half of the psychologists who work in mental hospitals have a PhD. Furthermore, many psychological services can be adequately rendered by persons with training at the MA level, especially if the organization of the psychological services provides for regular supervision and consultation by persons trained at the doctoral level. The conceptual and research skills traditionally associated with the PhD will only be required for persons engaged in activities that provide a more comprehensive understanding of key administrative responsibilities, have major responsibility for consultation with other professionals or paraprofessionals, or for those with substantial research responsibilities.

An issue that is related to level of training, especially at the MA level is the dissertation or thesis requirements. We favor the scientist-professional model at the PhD level, but are considerably less sanguine with regard to the value of a Master's thesis for correctional psychologists at the MA level. It would seem that development of research consumers rather than research producers would be a more useful goal for MA level psychologists.

Locus of Training   127

In this area, we have already noted that there are relatively few courses related to crime, delinquency, and corrections currently offered by psychology departments, and until very recently, there were no fully developed training programs. A number of psychologists contribute to interdisciplinary training programs that are housed in sociology departments or in schools of criminology. Unfortunately, the psychologists who work in these programs are often cut off from their parent discipline, and this may limit their access to new developments within psychology that would be relevant for their work. Housing graduate programs in crime, delinquency, and corrections within psychology departments would have certain advantages, but such programs would be deficient unless they included substantial inputs from other disciplines. For programs housed within psychology departments, the student has a clearer and perhaps more comfortable professional identity, and is more likely to be conversant with aspects of psychology that may be neglected in interdisciplinary programs. The training received in an interdisciplinary program in crime, delinquency and corrections, however, is likely to be more relevant and more immediately useful for the graduate of such programs. At this point in time, as previously noted, a diversity of models should be encouraged, both in psychology departments and in interdisciplinary settings.

Within psychology, there is no reason why graduate programs in crime, delinquency and corrections could not be developed as were clinical psychology training programs beginning over two decades ago. The needs are great, and more and more funds are being made available to produce professionals who can help combat the problems of crime and delinquency. However, with the possible exception of the recently created doctoral program at the University of Alabama, there are no programs to our knowledge housed entirely within psychology that offer a PhD with specialization in crime, delinquency or corrections. A number of programs seem to be moving toward the development of a subspecialty within these fields, within the broader context of a doctoral training program in clinical psychology. In the final section of this paper, we will describe, in some detail, our own efforts in developing a subspecialty in crime and delinquency in the doctoral training program in clinical psychology at Florida State University.

Interdisciplinary Relationships

Whatever the level, locus, or the type of training, close working relationships must be developed with correctional institutions, law enforcement agencies, the courts, and with probation and parole officers. As the focus of efforts in the criminal justice fields continues to shift to rehabilitation, the psychology of crime and delinquency will have increasing overlap with the field of community psychology. Indeed, in the not too distant future, it is foreseeable that community psychology will provide the umbrella under which

128   various subspecialties such as clinical psychology, school psychology, counseling psychology, correctional psychology, etc., will flourish. There are already a number of obvious common elements in these programs, such as a foundation in general psychology, an emphasis upon psychological evaluation, a concern with behavior change through counseling, psychotherapy, or behavior modification techniques, and the need to develop better instruments and research methodologies to deal with complex theoretical issues. It is also apparent that social psychology and other social science disciplines are extremely important for the professional psychologist in whatever setting he works, and that skills in psychological consultation and knowledge of social systems are more useful than knowledge of some of the traditional areas of psychology (e.g., animal learning).

The specific types of graduate programs in psychology that are developed will depend upon the interests of the psychology faculty, the resources of the department, and the existence of other related programs within the university, as well as the needs of society. The reaction to Sputnik gave us the resources to get on the moon, and the urgency of present problems in the areas of crime, delinquency, and corrections is likely to project a larger number of psychologists into the criminal justice system. It is, indeed, timely to be considering the nature of the graduate programs that should be developed.

ROLES AND PROBLEMS

The clinical psychologist as a scientist-professional can make a unique contribution to corrections and the criminal justice system. However, graduate students in clinical psychology rarely enter this field despite the many job opportunities that are available. Those who have entered often have found that they are poorly prepared to deal with the clinical and research problems encountered. The reason for this is that few students are exposed to offender populations in the course of their clinical training and virtually none are provided with systematic training in the area.

The new PhD typically seeks a position in which he can deal with the same clinical and research problems in which he became interested predoctorally. A graduate student who becomes involved in the treatment and study of schizophrenia, is likely to seek a position in a psychiatric institution where he can continue to pursue this interest. Because clinical students infrequently work with delinquents or criminals, or become involved in research using such populations, few consider employment in the criminal justice system unless all other alternatives have been exhausted. Those who do enter the system are often poorly prepared to cope realistically with the problems of such a setting. Typically they fall back on techniques for working with middle class neurotics or seriously disturbed psychotics—techniques that are inappropriate for coping with many justice clients.

The typical problems encountered by psychology students (and staff) in justice agencies, arise because of new role demands. Examples of constraints with which the psychology student has not been prepared to handle in his academic coursework are seen in the following trends: in the area of treatment, emphasis on the team approach in working with inmates, and an increasing need for knowledge of the legal rights of offenders; in terms of conducting research, the emphasis on protecting research subjects in correctional settings, needs and demands by justice administrators for more practical and relevant research, and an increasing agency research sophistication (or at least familiarity, which unfortunately leads to unrealistic expectations). While some of the following problems are not peculiar to psychology students, they seem to occur with alarming frequency; these are the common problems.

Typical Problem Areas

1. Lack of accurate information concerning the offender, i.e., typical life styles, home environment, past history, and effect of his contacts with the justice system.
2. Lack of accurate information concerning agency staff, i.e., who they are, their values, job demands, and perceptions of the agency and its clients.
3. Lack of information concerning institutional life, i.e., what happens to people crowded together in one setting, the authority relationships, the subcultural processes.
4. Difficulties in functioning as a member of a treatment team.
5. Lack of empathy for police and correctional officers, and other line staff.
6. Communication problems with other staff.
7. Problems in adapting to organizational requirements, i.e., internal regulations, dress standards, contraband.
8. Naivete concerning legal constraints upon him, and other staff members.
9. Lack of appreciation for immediate, practical problems that impinge on his freedom of professional options.
10. Little, if any, experience or training in conducting applied research within a field setting.
11. Lack of experience in therapy and testing with disadvantaged clients.
12. Lack of appreciation for lay therapists.
13. Tendency to avoid "problem inmates" and to select interesting inmates for therapy, i.e., those who share similar values.
14. Over-identification, at times, with clients versus staff.
15. Tendency to be taken in (conned) too easily with a resultant lack of respect by other staff members.
16. Unwillingness to work within the system to bring about a change in that system.
17. Missing the "big picture" because of an overly narrow view, i.e., psychol-

130   ogy has the answers.

18. A naive expectation that possession of an academic degree will result in immediate acceptance of ideas put forth.

19. A readiness to withdraw into comfortable roles and wait for requests for service rather than getting "into" the agency and finding out what programs and which personnel need help.

20. Lack of knowledge in dealing with administrative problems, such as budgets, personnel, as well as a lack of training in how to function as an "internal consultant."

GRADUATE PROGRAM AT FLORIDA STATE UNIVERSITY

Rationale and Goals

The goal of the FSU program is to provide specialty training in correctional psychology to students working toward the PhD in clinical psychology. In a recent statement, Jerris Leonard (1971), LEAA administrator, emphasized the importance of training clinical psychologists to work directly with offenders. We agree, but feel that it is equally important that the modern correctional psychologist should be a trained researcher as well as a practitioner. It is a sad fact that in criminal justice not only is there a lack of answers, but there is only a beginning in asking the appropriate questions. A practitioner learning the methods used today will be obsolete in 5 or 10 years unless he is also equipped with research skills to help develop the techniques for tomorrow.

Given the particular resources of the psychology department at the Florida State University, we feel that the major contribution that we can make to the manpower problems in the correctional area is to produce PhD level clinical psychologists in the scientist-professional tradition. They should have an opportunity to specialize in correctional psychology, to become cognizant of the academic work in the area and the approaches of other disciplines, to work with correctional psychologists, case workers, and custodial personnel in the treatment and rehabilitation of offenders in various settings, and to become sophisticated in the types of research best suited to such settings. This would be achieved through a specialty program which is integrated with an established doctoral training program in clinical psychology, drawing freely upon the resources of the Law School, Sociology Department, and the Department of Criminology.

Sequence of Study

The current specialty program in correctional psychology consists of shaping the requirements of the regular doctoral program in clinical psychology to maximize exposures to offender populations and justice system problems. During the first year of graduate study, the correctional specialty

student takes the regular sequence of courses required for all clinical students.
However, for his research apprenticeship he is assigned to one of the faculty
doing research relevant to correctional psychology. It is not uncommon for
students to carry out a project of their own during this first year. As part of
the fourth quarter clinical clerkship, the correctional student is often
assigned to the nearby Federal Correctional Institution (FCI) where he does
assessment work with youthful offenders.

During the second year of clinical training, the student decides on a
master's project and forms an MA committee. Students in the correctional
program embark on a research project relevant to this area. Some studies
relate directly to applied problems in criminal justice. Others investigate more
basic personality processes relating to theoretical issues in aggression or
psychopathy. Because of the unique cooperative training and research relationship that has developed between the FSU Psychology Department and the
Federal Correctional Institution, most students in the correctional psychology
specialty program carry out their masters' projects at the FCI.

The second year is also devoted to intensive training in psychological
assessment including a supervised clinical practicum. Students in the correctional program are assigned to the FCI for one of their practicum placements
unless they have already had their summer clerkship there. Other placements
in the rotation are selected to broaden the student's clinical experiences.
Those most relevant to the correctional program are the Marianna School, a
residential facility for delinquent boys, and the Albany, Georgia, Regional
Youth Center.

During the second and third years, students typically satisfy the PhD
language requirement. Most do so by passing the Princeton Exam in one
language and taking a 12 hour minor in another department. For the correctional student, these 12 hours are chosen so as to broaden his exposure to
how other disciplines approach the problems of deviance. Typically one or
two sociology courses and some courses in Criminology and Corrections are
selected focusing on theories of delinquency, sociological approaches to
deviance, race relations and criminal justice.

The third year is devoted to training in psychotherapy with clinical
students assigned to one of the local facilities for supervised therapy experience. Correctional students are assigned to the FCI. During the third year,
they also form a doctoral committee and select a topic for their critical
review paper. Once again, this paper should deal with a topic relevant to
correctional psychology. During this period, students also take those courses
offered which are relevant to their specialty whenever they are offered.

In the fourth year (or in some cases the fifth) students go on a one
year clinical internship. Correctional students are encouraged not to seek
internships in correctional setting justice agencies. The rationale for this is
that they will be receiving a substantial amount of pre-doctoral experience in

criminal justice settings. Post-doctorally, they will probably be seeking staff positions in such settings. Therefore, the internship probably represents their last opportunity to broaden their clinical experience.

Following the internship, students typically return to FSU to complete their dissertations. During this year the correctional students are employed as full-time psychology trainees at the Federal Correctional Institution, Tallahassee. The Bureau of Prisons has allocated four GS-9 level traineeships to the FCI. Graduate students in these positions work as staff psychologists, serving on classification and treatment teams, doing therapy and evaluations, consulting with FCI personnel, and supervising the assessment activities of second year practicum students. They themselves are supervised by the regular bureau of staff psychologists as well as by university personnel who serve as consultants.

Future Developments

Among the major assets of the program has been the good use made of available resources and practica facilities. As the program develops, it is planned to extend the field experiences of students to other correctional institutions, juvenile correctional settings, half-way houses, community agencies, and law enforcement departments. Visiting professors and consultants will be brought from outside as well as within psychology for expanding the viewpoint and knowledge bases of the students.

A final observation concerns the acceptance by the University. The development of the program, internally and from external recognition and support, has convinced the administration of its value. Thus, the program has not only been accepted by the University, but has received substantial fiscal support and administrative commitment.

SUMMARY

National concern about crime and delinquency problems has been increasing, as has professional psychology's felt responsibility to deal with social problems and issues. One of the results has been the development of graduate programs and subspecialties to prepare psychologists for working in justice agencies and with problems of law-violation and criminality. The programs are designed to remove impediments for effective involvement, some of which arise out of unfamiliarity with justice agency functioning and principles, and some of which are attributable to narrowness of professional preparation and knowledge.

These graduate programs train correctional and justice agency psychologists at the Bachelor's, Master's and PhD levels. They have all been initiated within the past five years. The programs represent a variety of models, all growing in size, and it seems likely that many more will be started.

The Florida State University program was described in some detail, not   133
as the single answer, but rather as a framework for comparison and discussion. In this program, a working relationship with a nearby Federal Correctional Institution and a careful academic integration with on-going curricula were seen as a basis for offering students considerable experience and perspective.

This chapter represents a first look at emerging graduate education in psychology in relation to problems of crime, delinquency and corrections. The attention that has been directed toward other areas in psychological education is now appropriate for this content area, as correctional psychology comes of age.

Behavior Sciences and Social Policies

The application of behavior sciences to justice systems can be viewed as taking place on a molecular or on a molar scale. Molecular study focuses on relatively small objective units of behavior. Findings from this process are fragmentary, isolated, and rarely generalized to larger phenomena.

Molar study, on the other hand, is associated with total, ongoing behavior according to its purposes and general meaning. For example, in direct service applications, public health models are molar in nature. They are concerned with large systems, patterns in these systems, and how these affect individuals and groups in terms of their medical and personal functioning.

One determinant of the behavioral scientists' activity along this continuum may be indicated by his point of intervention in the criminal justice process and by the number of persons he affects directly and indirectly. Thus, in public health practice, early intervention may affect large numbers of people by preventing spread of disease. Applied to psychological problems in the case of justice, the molar approach is to deal with social policy issues. The molar concern with social problems thus encompasses the outlooks of both the social activist and the system-challenger that have been discussed earlier. Adoption of the molar view entails, in many cases, changing principles and objectives that guide justice agencies, re-examining and modifying laws, and changing inputs, processes, and outputs.

For most behavioral scientists, social policy changes are beyond a professional arm's reach. To a few, these social policies are amenable only to

136 touching, rather than molding. In the broadest perspective, Skinner (1971) suggests that culture needs to be intentionally designed by changing the conditions which produce behavior. Cultural survival is seen as dependent upon benevolent, reciprocal control of man through behavior technologies. The technological view and the scope of the present discussion are much more limited, but the theme is similar; strategies can be developed from the social and behavioral sciences for influencing justice roles, conditions, and policies that shape human lives.

The scope of the behavior studied is related to the issue: what does one do with behavioral science information related to societal problems? And, what should behavioral scientists with strong feelings about social problems do? Three possible answers to these questions are: first, they should work in organized professional groups as behavioral scientists; second, they should work privately as individuals, not as behavioral scientists; third, they should seek employment as behavioral scientists in the social problem area or institution under study.

Miller (1972) presents a number of ways in which organized psychology has assumed an activist stance with respect to molar concerns of unemployment, nuclear explosions, racial discrimination, and police mistreatment of demonstrators. Over a dozen psychological societies have been specifically formed to deal with social problems. Reiff (1970) argues that organized psychology has a deep responsibility to influence public policies to help solve social crises and to promote human welfare. However, this type of involvement remains controversial. Scholarly or professional societies question both the potential impact and the appropriateness of the role.

The second choice is that psychologists and other behavioral scientists should speak out only as individuals, not as scientists. According to this view, "social reform, however justifiable or necessary, is not an appropriate role for a scientist or professional acting in those capacities [Miller, 1972] ." Such roles are seen as undermining psychology as a scholarly discipline.

The last choice noted is that behavioral scientists and mental health professionals should be actively involved in areas related to their own expertise and interests. This does not have to take place through professional organizations; an effective way of promoting social change is through direct professional and scientific activity. In the following section, attention is directed toward ways in which these social reform roles have been implemented. A number of cases will be considered. In some instances, the scientist-professional role has been part of a much larger social reform process, and consequently, cause-and-effect relationships cannot be observed. In other cases, the primary moving forces have been behavioral scientists and professionals; they represent models for such intervention.

The potential participation in public policy decisions may depend upon the conceptual breadth of the psychologists. The choice of the method of intervention can influence the final effect. Simon (1970) points out that unfamiliarity with non-psychological formulations from other disciplines interferes with effective social policy contributions. He states:

> In effect, we do not have a sound basis for an appropriate choice among interventions, for we tend . . . to apply psychological formulations without even considering the possibility that other analyses might be more suitable.

This type of disciplinary provincialism diverts attention from fundamental social problems. Simon cites as an example an attempted explanation of student unrest as a manifestation of the Oedipus Complex. To counteract this professional narrowness, students, scientists, and practitioners should be exposed to the contributions from the disciplines of law, sociology, social anthropology, government, and economics. If the psychologist's perspectives are thus broadened, his contributions to justice policies may be meaningful and just.

DECRIMINALIZATION

All socially deviant behavior is not illegal, nor is all anti-social behavior defined as crime. The processes by which behaviors become subsumed under the criminal law have resulted in a wide range of moral judgments becoming intertwined with the necessity for law enforcement. Indeed, the intolerance for social deviance in any society is apt to be directly proportional to the amount of crime.

Morris and Hawkins (1970) suggest that in the United States there is a massive overreach of the criminal law. They state: "Public sacrifice, throwing virgins off the rock, to reinforce the group superego, to placate the ancient gods, is not the job of the criminal justice system." They see criminal law as operating inefficiently, having been diverted from the goals of protecting property and persons by an unjustified involvement in private morality. Further, Morris and Hawkins point out that legislative actions create crime, by defining it. Sometimes this happens on a very wide scale, as in the case of the Volstead Act. The process is reversible; behavior can be decriminalized just as it can be criminalized.

If one agrees that far too many behaviors have been criminalized, then a major social policy implication becomes clear. The process by which so many actions and individuals become funnelled into the justice system must be changed. One immediate consequence this suggests is that scientists and professionals should direct their efforts at narrowing the range of behaviors that are defined as crime.

Behavioral scientists may foster this redefinition through advocacy, research, and direct action. The first priority in the delinquency area according to the federal Interdepartmental Coordinating Council (1972), is the removal of status offenses (truancy, runaways, stubborn children, etc.) from

138 the jurisdiction of the juvenile justice system. The Council further suggests that federal monies be withheld from juvenile delinquency programs until recipient jurisdictions follow this policy. This objective has grown out of the active participation and planning of psychologists, sociologists and other scientists. In addition, the decision was partially based upon research studies which indicated that more severe consequences result from a juvenile being adjudicated "in need of supervision," than his being adjudicated delinquent for serious crimes.

DEINSTITUTIONALIZATION

Several states, including Hawaii, Minnesota, and Massachusetts, have begun to close their prisons. Massachusetts closed all of its large traditional institutions for delinquent youth in 1972. The more than 2,000 youths who would normally have been confined in them during the year, were targeted instead for group homes (1,000), foster homes (200), youth advocacy (intensive counseling and referral services) (360), intensive casework (100), volunteer programs (600), a "Homeward Bound" program of outdoor survival (600), and secure intensive care for disturbed or dangerous youths (100).

The report of the Department of Youth Services (1972) indicates that the project was developed through several steps in the collaboration between behavioral research and planning, and legislative action. First, a series of five studies made by task forces and committees from 1965 to 1967 were critical of the Massachusetts Division of Youth Services; this provided a backdrop for change. Second, studies suggested that the institutions were costly, inhumane, and inefficient. Third, a new commissioner, Dr. Jerome G. Miller, a social worker by training, was appointed. Fourth, a bill was passed by the Massachusetts Legislature permitting very flexible use of funds, including grants-in-aid to cities for delinquency prevention, and purchase of outside services. And last, a decentralized community-oriented structure was created for administering the youth.

This social policy change was created through the recognition of the problem as defined by behavioral scientists, administrative willingness to change, and legislative action.

POINTS FOR INTERVENTION

A recurrent theme in the examination of both mental health and justice agencies concerns the best way to allocate available resources. The administrative decision reflects the skills and interests of the employees, the agency needs, and, occasionally, longitudinal baseline information on clients and problems. Two examples of longitudinal behavioral research with major policy implications are the Gottfredson base expectancy parole (1970) studies and the Wolfgang Philadelphia Cohort Study (1971).

Gottfredson (1970) found that much of the variance in parole success resulted from a few objective, biographical factors, such as opiate use in case history, prior commitments, type of offense, and age. Among other implications of this finding are that even with no clinical assessment, good parole prediction information is available, and that parole boards need to make judgments that take actuarial predictions into account.

In a study of 10,214 Philadelphia youngsters, Sellin, Wolfgang, and Figlio (1972) and Thornberry (1971) found that 35% had at least one police contact, 20% had at least two, 13% had at least three and 9% had at least four. Of the 3,475 with one contact, 1,485 (or 46%) had no subsequent police contact. This study suggests that many boys mature or change sufficiently that early clinical intervention would be a waste of effort in terms of preventing future police contact. The boys with continued police contacts would be the most appropriate targets for community or professional intervention. When intervention is made in early delinquency, an apt metaphor is "tiger prevention" (Zimring, 1970). Just as a man snapping his fingers on the streets of New York City doesn't keep tigers away ("You don't see any, do you?"), the youth worker does not prevent much delinquency recidivism. It just happens coincidentally that there are not many tigers or recidivists around.

THE PROBATION SUBSIDY PROGRAM

In 1966, the State of California instituted the Probation Subsidy Program as part of a deliberate strategy to promote the maintenance of offenders in their home counties. The state paid counties up to $4,000 per individual *not* sent to a state correctional institution. This pay scale was established from a base rate of institutionalization of offenders from each participating county. The money had to be used for either probation services or local programs for these offenders. After an initial flush of success, the program has had difficulties—in part from the use of the base rate of institutionalization. Nevertheless it represents a substantial modification of policy decisions resulting from economic and behavioral incentives.

This project is an outgrowth of Warren's (1967) Community Treatment Project. In that project, youthful offenders were differentially assigned to community treatment counselors according to the best outcome combinations of the two parties. Small caseloads and close attention to the matching process, resulted in the majority of these youths being successfully treated in the community. The subsidy program demonstrates the practicality of legislators, correctional administrators, and behavioral scientists working jointly for agreed goals that change institutions and societal procedures.

CONCLUSION

When psychologists enter the arena where other experts are already offering solutions to social policy issues, they run the risk of having valid ideas "dismissed as being commonplace [Margolin, 1972] " or being accused of using obscure jargon. Given these risks, why bother?

If the psychologist answering the question has not consumed his daily maintenance dose of "humble pills," his answer might be, "If not me, then who?" That is, among the number of knowledgeable people who are attempting to cope with society's complex crime and justice problems, the psychologist can do more than diddle with his Chi Squares. If he can forsake the comfortable role of observer of molecular events, he can become a prime influence on public policies in the justice system.

Some
Question Marks

A discussion of substantive achievement and possible contributions of psychology to justice has the risk of seeming like "The Big Picture," the Army's old television show. A military band beats out the strong vibrant sounds of a John Philip Sousa March; the outnumbered underdog is extraordinary in saving the victory and working for a brighter tomorrow; and the announcer, in a sonorous bass voice, solemnly declares that progress marches on.

Of course, when the band is not playing, there is a negative side to the involvement of behavioral science professionals with justice systems. Indeed, there is always another side. Some of the negative aspects include failures which remain privy only to those few intimately involved. They are never published or publicized; often, they are rationalized or hidden away to be forgotten as rapidly as possible. There are worse kinds of failures: those that are not recognized by the participants, or those obsolete procedures which are continued because of organizational inertia.

The research and professional involvements within ineffective programs are not necessarily culpable. Indeed, when the title "Some Grand Failures" was considered for this chapter, that title seemed inappropriate because it over-generalized about research and professional results; negative findings themselves may yield useful information. Instead, the "question marks" that are discussed here refer to on-going professional and scientific activities that are either currently under careful examination or need such scrutiny if they

142 are to be continued in their present form.

In this discussion, name-calling is not intended. It is not suggested that mental health professionals and behavioral scientists are maliciously or deliberately harming others or promoting inappropriate programs; nor is it suggested that they are incompetent or uninformed. These professionals may be captives of procedures that give them no choice. Rather, these question marks refer to some major social policy areas, relating to the organization of professional services. If any fault is to be found, it is in the perpetuation of unexamined procedures.

THE PREDICTION OF DANGEROUSNESS

A mechanism in both criminal and civil law for depriving individuals of their freedom is the attribution of "dangerousness." Although dangerousness is frequently defined as threatening the property, welfare, or safety of others or oneself, in actuality, there is much of this sort of dangerousness that is not subsumed under the criminal law. For example, the football player and the professional boxer are individuals who selectively interfere with the safety of others in ways that are societally approved.

When individuals come under the auspices of one of the justice systems, mental health professionals are often asked for evaluations of dangerousness. At that point, dangerousness is treated as a clinical phenomenon, isolated from the context of social problems and situations. Typically, dangerousness is not explicitly defined. The underlying meaning as described by Sarbin (1967), is a threat to the status quo or existing power structure, within a role-system. This view rules out dangerousness as the expression of a personality trait.

The problems in defining dangerousness are: (a) There seems to be no such behavioral entity as dangerousness, that mental health professionals (or others) can define, apart from social contexts or attitudes. To predict the likely commission of a specific offense, such as murder, is very difficult, but does specify the target behavior. This need for examining observable, specific units of behavior extends to all areas of assessment. Crary and Steger (1972) stated:

> While psychological tests have apparently poor validity for inferring high-order states and traits, this does not mean they may not have utility for reaching decisions which require more objective observations or lower order inferences.

(b) There is limited knowledge about base rates of certain types of "dangerousness," such as battery, in the general population. When a professional judgment is made about such behavior for a specific event, the likelihood of occurrence for any population is needed for comparative purposes. (c) The statistical prediction of any rare event, such as an aggressive threat to safety, is a difficult burden for any professional to assume. (d) In making these kinds of judgments, an estimate has to be made of the acceptable fail rate. By judging almost everyone as dangerous and keeping them in institutions, it is possible to have a zero rate of commission of the undesirable behavior. By designating very few as dangerous, by whatever criteria, a much higher risk and fail rate will accrue. A judgment has to be made of the acceptable risk rate to be assumed by the predictor, and indirectly, by society.

The prediction of dangerousness becomes an especially important issue in view of the 1966 *Baxstrom v. Herald* decision (383 U.S. 107). The United States Supreme Court ruled that proper judicial procedures had not been followed in the civil commitment of Johnnie K. Baxstrom to a New York Department of Corrections security hospital from completion of his prison sentence. As a result, 969 persons were released or transferred to civil hospitals. Most of these had been judged as "dangerous" in psychiatric and psychological examinations. In a follow-up study, only seven of these released patients were potentially harmful or difficult enough to warrant subsequent commitment to a security hospital. Hunt and Wiley (1968) concluded their report on the Baxstrom case with the observation: "This would appear to be another instance of institutionalized expectations putting blinkers on our perceptions."

Thus, major questions arise about the overprediction of "dangerousness" by mental health professionals as inappropriately restricting the liberty of many persons. Indeed, by some definitions, many mental health professionals themselves are dangerous. Surely the time has come for a moratorium on dangerousness predictions made without consideration of statistical base rates, specification of target behavior, and determinations of acceptable fail rates. Additional considerations include the expectations promoted by the person's environment, effects of degree of distress, the setting in which the person will be, and finer differentiation among types of people considered likely to commit specific offenses.

CLINICAL INJUSTICE

Among the possible destructive effects of attaching to people psychiatric or psychological labels is the development of self-fulfilling negative prophesies. The general principle that groups respond to social labels which sometimes results in an impairment of the future of those labeled, applies to justice systems.

There are some special characteristics of psychological labeling and clinical involvement in justice systems. Laws have been enacted which follow psychiatric diagnostic terminologies and beliefs. There are sexual psychopath laws, defective delinquent laws, and others which identify special treatment, sentencing, and the creation of institutions based on these diagnostic findings. Indeed, if we accept the belief that the term mental illness was intended as a metaphor, then we now have the codifying and criminalization of this reified

144 metaphor. Thus large amounts of criminal justice power now come under the leaky umbrella of mental health principles. And while they are assumed with good intent, one outcome is longer sentences under conditions of minimum treatment and higher restrictions on freedom than the same individuals would otherwise receive serving prison sentences. The idealist treatment philosophy has become an albatross around the necks of those enmeshed in the system. Kittrie (1971) suggests that in this process, the "therapeutic state" offers few of the traditional legal safeguards against societal abuses.

One setting in which good intentions sometimes become bad consequences, is the juvenile justice system. The procedure of adjudicating individuals as delinquent was developed to permit youths humane, non-criminal treatment. As this process often operates today, normal adolescent developmental problems are misidentified as psychiatric or criminologic difficulties. As a result, youths adjudicated as delinquent or incorrigible are sent to training schools that differ little in function or in appearance from penitentiaries. The implications of the Supreme Court 1966 *Kent v. U.S.* decision (383 U.S. 541), are that youths are entitled to full legal protection provided to adults in judicial proceedings.

Finally, these cautions and problems apply to research studies as well as direct services. Kahn (1965) has discussed this issue with respect to the use of the Glueck Social Prediction Table; in one application, the prediction of delinquency was seen as potentially far more harmful than helpful to the five and six year old boys who served as subjects. Similar cases may be found in every aspect of justice system research.

RECEPTION AND DIAGNOSTIC CENTERS:
THE EDSELS OF CORRECTIONS

When reception and diagnostic centers were first started in the United States in 1918, they were viewed as an extraordinary advancement. They were to serve two purposes. First, they were designed to sort out individuals, so that youthful, relatively unsophisticated offenders would not be contaminated by being incarcerated with confirmed criminals. Second, they were designed to provide a place for professional diagnosis so that individuals could be sent to institutions that offer the treatment they needed. This way of thinking about diagnosis assumed a medical process: identify what is wrong with the person, then apply the appropriate treatment. This thinking further assumed that staff would be present to provide these services at the destination institutions.

These high expectations have been followed by an Edsel-like flop. Diagnostic centers have not worked. Some of the classification functions have been satisfactory from a management point of view in offering a centralized place for client assessment and educational testing. But the elaborate, expensive and time consuming diagnoses that are made are typically a waste of time. Founded on an illness model of criminality, they often bear little relationship to the circumstances leading to the individual being defined as an offender. Furthermore, even for individuals specifically in need of psychological treat ment, there is a functional isolation of therapy recommendations from treat ment services. Reception and diagnostic centers tend to be better staffed than the settings to which the individuals are sent. For the few destination insti tutions in which adequate treatment services are offered, the recommendations are often ignored; a separate assessment is made which fits the frame of refer ence of the treaters.

Large numbers of professionals at reception and diagnostic centers find themselves performing boring, repetitive tasks; staff turnover is large; the staff members are frustrated, both by not being able to follow through them selves on recommendations and in the inability of the destination institu tions to offer treatment services. Finally, there is little feed-back on what is accomplished. As diagnoses are made of an unending procession of offenders, staff become increasingly routinized and institutionalized. This waste of staff is inexcusable in a justice system where mental health professionals have been at a premium. Nevertheless correctional systems persist in planning and build ing new diagnostic centers—next year's Edsels.

PSYCHIATRIC TREATMENT PROGRAMS IN PRISON

In prison, psychiatric treatment programs may be subjected to two questions. First, should they be there? Second, when they are applied, do they work? The Patuxent Institution discussed earlier has had mixed results. How ever, this is not a typical prison nor does it deal with typical clients.

Rollin (1969) has discussed the failure of the British Mental Health Act of 1959. Under this act, large numbers of unprosecuted as well as convicted "mentally abnormal offenders" were admitted to mental hospitals. Rollin's evaluation was that this commitment of "dangerous" men to mental hospitals was nonsense, and that the promises for psychiatric procedures in helping these offenders were overstated. His study reports:

> It is my opinion that the tools of psychiatry are blunt and primitive and in fact are largely ineffectual when used on the general body of mentally abnormal offenders we are called upon to treat [Rollin , 1969] .

Two longitudinal studies are relevant. Jacobson and Wirt (1969) con ducted follow-up studies of group psychotherapy in the Minnesota State Prison. A total of 446 inmates over a period of eight years were seen in group psychotherapy, in 40 separate groups, by 26 different therapists. In addition, there were 300 volunteers in 34 control groups and other control groups for individuals who refused to volunteer. Jacobson and Wirt reported that, overall, the controls made a somewhat better adjustment to parole than the

146   groups in psychotherapy.

In the most comprehensive study to date, Kassebaum, Ward, and Wilner (1971) studied groups that underwent either mandatory or voluntary group counseling. A total of 955 subjects from one California prison were followed for 36 months after parole. Of those with available follow-up data, 68 had been in mandatory large group counseling, 171 in mandatory small group counseling, and 274 in voluntary small group counseling. A mandatory control group had 269 subjects and a voluntary control group had 173 subjects. Failure was defined in terms of either law violation, conviction, and sentencing to more than 90 days, or parole violation and subsequent return to prison. The failure rates in the counseling treatment groups were 70%, 57% and 60%, respectively, and the failure rates in the two control groups were 58% and 66%. No significant differences emerged in the parole outcomes or in degree of conformity to staff values.

These studies do not suggest that there is no role for psychological and psychiatric programs in prison. They do strongly indicate that attention needs to be directed selectively; the question is, to whom, under what circumstances, and with what kind of treatment.

BLACKS AND OTHER MINORITY GROUPS IN THE CRIMINAL JUSTICE SYSTEM

Blacks in America have a higher probability than whites of having involvement with the police; once having made contact, they have a greater likelihood of being arrested, of being arraigned, of being convicted, and of being sent to prison. This accounts, in part, for the substantial numbers of Blacks—well out of proportion to the nation's population—that are clients in the justice system. Staff of these agencies contain fewer Blacks proportionately. Bitterness, resentment, and the feeling among Black justice clients that prison is a continuation of the whtie man's discrimination, are not unusual. The situation is the same for Chicanos, Indians, and Puerto Ricans.

Have mental health professionals and behavioral scientists participated in public policy decisions which will alter this imbalance? Will they be able to influence social, economic and political forces to help change this state of being? Can the behavioral sciences find methods for providing opportunities for minority groups to achieve their goals through legitimate means, increase their commitments to conventional activities, build generalized bonds to society, and promote a sufficient level of satisfaction so that many of the social problems will no longer exist? These are démanding tasks. But to wait, along with the other disciplines until all are ready, prolongs the problem, and rationalizes the current state of relative inaction.

SUMMARY

Every professional and scientist working in a justice agency carries his own mental file of question marks. The above suggestions represent an incomplete list of problem areas. Nevertheless, the implications seem clear. There are a number of ways in which mental health professionals and behavioral scientists influence both clients and criminal justice systems. To the extent we can conceptualize broader processes, our potential for the actualization of positive change increases. To the extent that our tunnel vision continues, these question marks will become, indeed, our grand failures.

Appendix A

Psychologists in Corrections —

Are They Doing Good for the Offender
or Well for Themselves?

David L. Bazelon

When President Johnson appointed the members of the Presidential Commission to study crime in America, there was a great hue and cry over the failure to name to the Commission a single behavioral scientist. I joined in the criticism because I had been assured by men whose intellect and judgment I admired that the behavioral sciences could provide a significant input to the Commission's effort. In response to the uproar, the Commission indicated that it had no intention of insulating itself from behavioral science. And at my urging, a meeting was called to establish a procedure whereby the contributions of these scientists could be funnelled into the project. I proposed this meeting not because I was in a position to define the role these sciences could fill, but because I saw myself as a spokesman for men and women who could sit down with the Commission and provide great help. Representatives of some of the leading associations in the field were present at the meeting.

The meeting could only be described as a calamity. I was disappointed and embarrassed that some of the outstanding scholars in these areas could not come up with anything resembling a workable program. In fact, to the best of my recollection, not a single significant idea or proposal emerged from the entire discussion. No one was able to describe the contributions these disciplines could make, or even to suggest a means of finding out what sort of contribution might be made. And more, no one was ready to accept an assignment to formulate a proposed course of action.

Regretfully, I must tell you that the papers prepared for this conference

150   on the role of psychology in corrections do nothing to allay my increasing doubts and uncertainties about what it is that psychologists or any other behavioralists can offer. All of the papers begin with the unexamined assumption that the correctional psychologist can make an important contribution, and the further assumption, which is thought to follow logically, that we therefore need more psychologists. None of them examines critically the work that psychologists have done in the past, or even begins to inquire why they have failed to accomplish more. There is no mention of changes in the training, practice or employment of the correctional psychologist. None of the papers even asks whether there should be any such specialty.

It would be easy to dismiss my doubts, of course, if the scholars at the meeting I described or those who prepared these papers were second-rate representatives of their profession. But correctional psychology has no more able spokesmen than these. I am not a psychologist and naturally I am not well qualified to evaluate their credentials. But from all accounts these men fully deserve their outstanding reputations. If these leaders have not yet established a role in this area for your profession, then there are difficult questions that must finally be confronted.

I certainly hope you will not draw the impression that I consider psychology a worthless discipline that ought to be abandoned. The issue is not whether psychology is good, but what it is good at. I think that I can make my point by telling you a story about a mother who called a doctor and told him that her young son was suffering terribly from fever, nausea, and cramps. "Is he having fits?" the doctor asked. The mother said no. "That's too bad," the doctor replied. "I'm terrific on fits." I am afraid that I may be addressing a large group of the nation's leading specialists on fits, who have been asked to treat a patient that badly needs care, but that doesn't happen to be suffering from fits. There is no doubt that our correctional apparatus is gravely ill. The question is, is your expertise—which no one questions—what we need to solve this particular problem?

On the whole, it seems to me that the institution of correctional psychology has had far too little outside evaluation or scrutiny. Psychologists have not produced any remarkable successes in the corrections field. But apparently that has never been considered a sufficient reason to scrutinize your work closely. After all, our entire correctional process is a shambles, and it is hard to single out psychologists for blame when none of the other participants has been able to generate successful programs. Moreover, psychology is still widely considered a fledgling discipline in the field of corrections, and it is often assumed that it needs breathing room and time to establish itself before it can make inroads on the problem. Demanding quick results could smother the effort, or encourage programs that sacrifice long-range promise for short-term pay-offs. And finally, even if we were prepared to hold psychologists to a stringent standard of accountability, we simply don't have any

uniformly agreed upon standard to measure your performance. To be sure, 151
there are critics like Dr. Thomas Szasz who tell you that you have no right to
succeed. But no one on the outside has been able to take psychology on its
own terms and ask whether it has moved the ball forward or provided data
which would enable others to begin understanding our problems. Accordingly,
if any questioning is to be done, you are the ones who must do it.

In suggesting that you initiate a process of self-criticism and re-examina-
tion, I cannot avoid the responsibility that I share with other judges and law
enforcement officials for having pressed you to assume your present role in the
correctional process. To a large extent you did not volunteer—you were
asked to come up with answers for problems that seemed too difficult for us
to solve. Perhaps I deserve a special share of the responsibility, for I have
devoted much of my career to the goal of opening lines of communication
between law and the social sciences. And I hope you will not depreciate my
questioning as the predictable over-reaction of a disenchanted lover. We all
have to learn some hard truths about uncritical reliance on experts. Difficult
problems will not go away merely because we turn them over to experts.
Throughout the criminal process one can find distressing examples of just that
kind of uncritical reliance. In the area of civil commitment, for example, the
courts have frequently abandoned to behavioral scientists and doctors the
responsibility for deciding which persons would be subject to involuntary
treatment. These experts are unquestionably knowledgeable about mental illness and various treatment modalities. But the questions raised by civil commitment are primarily legal and moral, not medical. And there is no reason to
assume that the expertise of these doctors and scientists extends to questions
of law and morality. Perhaps we should rely on these doctors, whatever their
expertise, to make the legal and moral decisions. But we clearly should not
stick our heads in the sand and pretend that we are only asking them medical
questions.

In the same vein, the courts and law enforcement agencies have often
tried to wash their hands of the correctional process, comforted with the
notion that the experts—you—are minding the store. That may be the
easy solution for us, and I am sure it has advantages for you, but it must not
stop us from asking whether the questions raised by crime and punishment
and corrections are really questions that psychologists or other behavioralists
can and should be answering.

Because the related problems of crime and corrections are deeply dis-
turbing to a large number of people, and because none of the attempted solutions show any sign of success, there is an almost irresistible temptation to
soothe the public by sweeping the problems under the rug. One method of
accomplishing this is to treat the courts as a whipping boy, blaming them for
a problem they did not create and they cannot solve. But a second method of
camouflaging the real issues—and the one that should concern us here—is

to divert the public's attention by calling on experts to provide a pill that will magically make all of our problems disappear. Instead of facing up to the true dimensions of the problem and admitting that violent crime is an inevitable by-product of our society's social and economic structure, we prefer to blame the problem on a criminal class—a group of sick persons who must be treated by doctors and cured. Why should we even consider fundamental social changes or massive income redistribution if the entire problem can be solved by having scientists teach the criminal class—like a group of laboratory rats—to march successfully through the maze of our society? In short, before you respond with enthusiasm to our plea for help, you must ask yourselves whether your help is really needed, or whether you are merely engaged as magicians to perform an intriguing side-show so that the spectators will not notice the crisis in the center ring. In considering our motives for offering you a role, I think you would do well to consider how much less expensive it is to hire a thousand psychologists than to make even a miniscule change in the social and economic structure. If your participation permits us to divert the public's attention by calling on experts to provide a pill that will holding out your skills as pertinent to the solution of the problem.

The critical issue, it seems to me, is whether the fundamental postulates of your discipline make it impossible for you to reach the central problem. Your discipline inevitably assumes, I think, that aberrent behavior is the product of sickness, and it brings to bear on the problem a medical or therapeutic model. That model assumes a white, middle-class, non-conforming subject whose anti-social conduct is attributable to mental disturbance. That type of subject may well be amenable to group therapy and the other rehabilitative techniques in your arsenal. It also assumes, and I think this emerges clearly from the papers prepared for this conference, that criminals are more like other criminals than they are like other human beings. I am hard pressed to see how those assumptions can be applied to the problem of violent crime— the kind of crime that most alarms society. That kind of crime is committed by persons who are clearly at the bottom of society's barrel. They have usually been raised in deplorable and destructive conditions with few of the values and goals that are usually pushed on middle-class children. We should not be surprised if a great many of them don't respond to the same pressures and stimuli that motivate middle-class children. I fear that we may be trying to rehabilitate these offenders with techniques that can work, if at all, only on the middle class. Poor, black offenders are not necessarily sick. They may simply be responding to an environment that has impoverised them, humiliated them and embittered them. Will group therapy help a black teenager who steals cars and peddles drugs, and who will be tossed at the end of his "rehabilitation" right back into the environment that nurtured him? Will the Rorschach or Bender-Gestalt tests tell us anything about the offender who steals, not because he suffers from kleptomania and get his "kicks" from stealing, but because he wants money to buy goods and services that most 153 of us can already obtain? Or one who needs money to satisfy his addiction to narcotic drugs? Does it really make sense to treat such an offender as a sick person who can be cured? Have we, perhaps, been focusing our attention on the wrong part of the problem—the offender and his mental condition instead of the conditions that produced him?

The papers presented at this conference carry the implication that these questions can be answered as soon as we have more programs, more of something labelled rehabilitation, and, above all, more psychologists. But if these requests for more are predicated on an unrealistic picture of the problem, then more of anything is not going to solve the problem. I am convinced, at least, that more money will not provide an answer. When I was on the Advisory Council of the National Institute of Mental Health I saw hundreds of project proposals that were designed to deal with these problems, but I think I could count on one hand the number that offered anything like promise of producing information useful to persons in the front lines of the criminal process. And research money is being squandered on action programs that have no connection with the real world. For example, we already have a penal institution in West Virginia that spends, and this was the figure several years ago, about $13,000 per year on each inmate. Don't we have to ask whether the problem could be better handled by letting the inmates out of the institution and just giving each one of them $13,000 per year? From what I understand about the theory that underlies that institution it seems to me outdated, and I cannot think of any function for it except as a warehouse for those offenders who are least in need of help (and who would probably have been released if this impressive facility were not available). I think we have to ask whether these elaborate and costly programs for research and rehabilitation serve any other function than providing staff—including correctional psychologists— with jobs and income. That is not an easy question for you to ask. But I do not see how—in good conscience—you can avoid it.

If I have given you the impression that I am convinced psychology has no role to play in this area, then I must clarify my own position. I don't know whether psychology should have a significant role, and I don't even know how to find out except by asking you. If you undertake the inquiry I am suggesting, you may reach the painful conclusion that you have completely misdirected your efforts in trying to solve the problems of crime and corrections. More likely, however, you will conclude that psychology does have a limited role, but that its potential abilities have been greatly overstated. That conclusion would be extremely important, for you cannot hold yourselves out as capable of solving the entire problem when you can have an impact, at best, on no more than a very, very small part of it—particularly as respects the kind of crime which causes the government to support such meetings as this one.

154   You may find, for example, that the therapeutic model does have application to certain kinds of white-collar crime, crimes of passion and mental illness rather than poverty and drug addiction. If that is your conclusion, then I urge you to pursue that aspect of the overall problem. Middle-class crime is a significant subject of inquiry, and your contribution will probably be important. But there should be no mistake that the crime problem which most alarms the public is not the problem of white-collar crime, but the problem of so-called violent street crime. And since the public is obsessed with violent street crime, it is willing to spend large amounts of money to ferret out a solution. If psychologists proclaim their inability to participate in the search, they will, of course, lose their share of the money. Conferences like this one probably could not take place without the financial support of a public that thinks you can help solve the problem of violent street crime. If you conclude that the problem is beyond your powers, we all may have to stay at home more often. But I am sure you will agree that there is no justification for obtaining public money—even for worthy purposes—under false pretenses. More important, so long as you permit us to talk about a magic pill instead of the real problem, we will seriously delay the quest for a meaningful solution.

Alternatively, you may find that you can have a significant impact on the problem of violent crime by taking bitter and violent offenders and reshaping them so that they learn to live with the devastating and ugly conditions of life that none of us could tolerate. If you can succeed in that endeavor, I am confident that the public will shower you with money and you will honestly have earned it. But whether you want to serve as high-priced janitors who sweep up society's debris so that our problems will be pushed out of sight but in no sense resolved, is a question that you yourselves must answer after you have squarely faced it.

Appendix B

Psychologists in Corrections
and Justice:

Another View

Lorrin M. Koran and Bertram S. Brown

When a jurist as qualified and eminent as Judge David Bazelon questions the role of psychology in the field of corrections, psychologists can be sure that the questions raised are important and penetrating ones. Judge Bazelon's written opinions and decisions have been a major force in opening the way for behavioral scientists to contribute to many critical questions encountered in the law and in legal processes. Among the many vital issues confronted in his decisions are how to estimate and define dangerousness (Cross v. Harris, 418 F2d 1095, 1969); the criteria for an insanity defense (Durham v. U.S., 214 F2d 862, 1954); the legal right to adequate treatment for persons who are involuntarily confined (Rouse v. Cameron, 373 F2d 451, 1966); and the right of psychologists to enter testimony before a court (Jenkins v. U.S., 307 F2d 637, 1962).

In his paper on psychologists in corrections, Judge Bazelon urges self-criticism and outside evaluation. He says the issue is what psychology is good at. He asks if "the questions raised by crime and punishment and corrections are really questions that psychologists . . . can and should be answering." He asks with regard to the offender who steals to satisfy a narcotic habit, "Does it really make sense to treat such an offender as a sick person who can be cured?" He states that, "Psychologists have not produced any remarkable successes in the corrections field." What can be said in reply?

156 CRITICISM AND EVALUATION

Criticism and evaluation of the roles of psychologists and psychological principles in corrections are needed and welcome. To paraphrase Socrates somewhat irreverently, "The unexamined profession is not worth practicing." In these early days of the application of psychological principles to the field of corrections, it is doubly important that evaluation be stressed in order to promote identified successes and prevent repetition of identified blunders. NIMH is currently funding a number of evaluative studies in this field and more would be welcome. For example, one investigator is comparing a community-based rehabilitative program for court-committed juvenile delinquents with a treatment program in correctional institutions. Another investigator is evaluating the effects of group psychotherapy on the rehabilitation of criminal sexual offenders. A third psychologist is evaluating the deterrent effectiveness of informal probation compared to formal probation.

WHAT PSYCHOLOGY IS GOOD AT

Compared to physics, astronomy or chemistry, psychology is a relatively young discipline, having separated itself gradually from philosophy only in the last century. Its subject matter—Man the social animal, the tool-making animal, the wise, the playful, the irrational, the cruel—is so much more complex than the laws of motion, the nature of the stars, or the properties of atoms, that it's far too early to expect a set of crystalline formulae which will describe and predict the behavioral vagaries of Man's reason, his emotions, and his will. On the other hand, in its short life, psychology has shown itself to be good at a number of things which may ultimately benefit the law and legal processes. Psychology is good at applying scientific methods to analyzing human behavior. It is good at formulating testable hypotheses and designing experiments to test them. A great deal of work has been done, for example, on the role of attitudes and expectations in shaping behavior. This work can be translated into changes in prison atmosphere and procedures or into methods of helping released offenders deal with community attitudes and expectations. Psychologists are good at evaluating an individual's intelligence, skills, aptitudes, and other assets and translating these assessments into individually tailored rehabilitative programs. These evaluations and programs could be helpful if more widely available in the correctional arena. Psychologists are good at identifying parental behaviors which help produce aggression and delinquency in children and in helping parents to curb these behaviors. They may be good at stimulating self-study by those involved in the criminal justice system. For example, one psychologist has recently helped a group of local police study officers frequently engaged in violent incidents and officers rarely engaged in such incidents to learn how violence can be prevented.

Psychologists have begun to move beyond their traditional concern with the   157
individual into studies of communities and social systems. Psychologists are
becoming good at working with school systems to help them reach children
who are academic failures or behavior problems, and with community agencies
to help them examine the impact of their procedures on potential clients.
Lest this rosy picture be accepted as a complete one, it should be quickly
added that psychologists in large numbers have not raced to apply their under-
standings to the correctional field or to carry out much needed research in
this area. Certainly psychologists as well as other behavioral scientists have
been somewhat reluctant to become deeply involved in the conceptual,
methodological, and policy bramble patches which surround most social
issues, including clarification of the frequently conflicting goals and objectives
found throughout the entire juvenile and criminal justice systems.

THE QUESTIONS RAISED BY CRIME AND PUNISHMENT AND CORRECTIONS

Are these "really questions that psychologists . . . can and should be
answering." Crime and punishment and corrections raise a host of questions.
Many of them, if not most, fall outside the competency of psychologists and
behavioral scientists and within the competence of jurists and other members
of professions within the legal system. But for at least some questions,
psychologists either can or should provide answers or partial answers.
Psychologists can help provide information on the internal and environmental
causes of criminal behavior. They can identify effects on the individual of
societal labelling of deviant behavior by terms such as "criminal" or "delinquent," or the effects on the social system of labelling certain behaviors as
deviant. They can help answer questions regarding the effectiveness of punishment or the likelihood that criminal sanctions written into law will serve as
deterrents. They can help answer questions regarding an individual offender's
assets and liabilities and the program of rehabilitation most likely to help
him. They can help provide police officers and corrections officials with
answers to questions about effective crisis intervention, about riot control and
the prevention of violence. As yet, psychologists' answers are not final or
definitive or complete. They cannot promise nor can they deliver a rose
garden. Still, they can help identify the conditions and the work needed for
the garden's growth.

THE PLACE OF THE SICKNESS MODEL

Judge Bazelon puts his finger on an ugly truth when he says that "Poor,
black offenders are not necessarily sick. They may simply be responding to an
environment that has impoverished them, humiliated them and embittered

158 them." The Judge is eminently correct: it is insufficient in this situation to merely treat the offender. He points out the need for fundamental social changes. We agree and we believe that psychologists and other behavioral scientists, both as professionals and as citizens, would agree. There is a need to move on both fronts—helping the victim of a damaging social environment and changing that environment. Just as in the past we treated the victims of water-borne cholera at the same time we moved to clean up water supplies, so it is necessary today to help the individual offender at the same time we move to change the social conditions which contribute to his criminal behavior. As citizen advocates with special knowledge about the effects of toxic social environments, psychologists with experience in the corrections system can vigorously lobby for social change. As members of the helping professions within the corrections system, they can lobby for an atmosphere of rehabilitation and prevention instead of one of vengeance. They can also help environmentally disadvantaged offenders challenge their environment, change it and master it instead of allowing it to poison them.

As a result of the decisions and opinions of Judge Bazelon and other distinguished jurists, the place of the sickness model in legal thinking is a matter of active debate. The debate is perhaps most lively with regard to the narcotic addict who is an offender. In Robinson v. California (370 U.S. 660, 1962), the Supreme Court held unconstitutional a California statute which made the status of being an addict a criminal status per se. The Court held that punishing an individual for suffering from the disease of addiction was a cruel and unusual punishment in violation of the Eighth Amendment. The wisdom of treating addiction rather than punishing it is becoming a recognized part of American public policy. The question of whether or not to punish addicts who engage in stealing or other property crimes in order to support their habits is receiving intensive study. Under the Narcotic Addict Rehabilitation Act of 1966 (P.L. 91-793), Congress allowed addicts charged with or convicted of violating certain Federal criminal laws to receive treatment for their addiction in lieu of prosecution or sentencing. NIMH now has underway an evaluative study to determine the effectiveness of this treatment policy in restoring the health of addicts and returning them to society as useful members unlikely to commit further crimes. The knowledge gained from this study should help the Congress and policy-makers at other levels of government determine how far and in what ways to extend public policies based on acceptance of narcotic addiction as a disease.

Of course, psychological theory and practice are not limited nor should they be to the sickness model of deviant behavior or to models based on internal drives, motives, and attitudes. Social psychological perspectives have been part of psychology for many years. Moreover, behavior modification programs, for example, can be based on relations between behavior and environmental conditions without considering the internal states of the

individual. Additional social psychological research, however, would be quite
helpful. For example, influences which bear on community tolerance of deviant behavior and on alternatives to handling deviant behavior by means of the criminal justice system appear to be fruitful areas for further exploration.

PSYCHOLOGISTS' SUCCESSES IN THE CORRECTIONS FIELD

With some qualification, Judge Bazelon's statement is correct that, "Psychologists have not produced any remarkable successes in the corrections field." Psychologists have not produced any *nationally adopted* remarkable successes in the corrections field. But a few examples of remarkable successes do exist. Psychologists in the California Youth Authority helped design and operate a system of community-based rehabilitation for court-committed juvenile delinquents which demonstrated that these young men and women could be maintained in the community without any higher recidivism than similar juvenile delinquents treated in correctional institutions. This study suggests that community-based programs can achieve results equal to institutional programs while costing less and causing less disruption in the lives of young offenders. A study at the Draper Correctional Center in Elmore, Alabama has shown that youthful offenders at the maximum security State prison can be motivated to complete high school or college-level education which may help them achieve a better life on release.

Unfortunately, however, there are not a large number of "remarkable successes." Psychologists enter the corrections process at a late stage in the development of the individual's criminal behavior. The offender has already offended, been caught, tried, convicted, sentenced and labelled a "criminal." Nonetheless, the need for increased participation on the part of psychologists and other behavioral scientists in the corrections system is acute. The high level of crime in American society makes it urgent that we intensively study means of preventing and correcting criminal behavior. We must also begin transferring what has been learned about other forms of deviant behavior and about human behavior in general to the field of corrections.

Despite the need for increased participation on the part of psychologists and other behavioral scientists, Judge Bazelon is correct in suggesting that the role of psychologists in the corrections system is likely to be a limited one. They are not capable of solving the full problem by themselves. They do not possess a magic pill to prevent or cure criminal behavior. What is needed is a rich brew of resources, talents, research, training, changed social attitudes toward crime and punishment, and the distillation of that brew into action programs at every level of the correctional system. The brew will not come into being by itself. Only the political activity of the public can bring it into being. For this to occur, public attitudes toward offenders must change away from the fear, hate, indifference and hopelessness which have marked these

160   attitudes in the past. Fortunately, this change seems to be developing. As it progresses, it seems clear that psychologists should participate in the development of the resulting nutrient brew. It seems equally clear that at every step of the brewing process, hard questions, penetrating questions, thoughtful questions asked by Judge Bazelon and other distinguished participants in the legal process are a welcome and necessary seasoning.

References

CHAPTER ONE

Abrahamsen, D. *The psychology of crime.* New York: Science Editions, 1960.

Alexander, F., & Staub, H. *The criminal, the judge, and the public.* New York: Macmillan, 1931.

Barnes, H. E., & Teeters, N. K. *New horizons in criminology.* Englewood Cliffs, N.J.: Prentice-Hall, 1959.

Corsini, R. J., & Miller, G. A. Psychology in prisons, 1952. *American Psychologist,* 1954, **9**, 184-185.

Glueck, S., & Glueck, E. T. Five hundred criminal careers. New York: Knopf, 1930.

Gross, H. *Criminal psychology: A manual for judges, practitioners, and students.* Boston: Little, Brown and Company, 1911.

Healy, W. *Honesty: A study of the causes and treatment of dishonesty among children.* Indianapolis: Bobbs-Merrill, 1915.

Healy, W., Bronner, A. F., Baylor, E. M. H., & Murphy, J. P. *Reconstructing behavior in youth.* New York: Knopf, 1929.

Healy, W., & Healy, M. T. *Pathological lying, accusation, and swindling.* Boston: Little, Brown and Company, 1915.

Hearnshaw, L. S. *A short history of British psychology 1840-1940.* New York: Barnes and Noble, 1964.

Karpman, B. *Case studies in the psychopathology of crime: A reference*

162   *source for research in criminal material.* New York: The Mental
      Science Publishing Company, 1933.

Kolasa, B. J. Psychology and law. *American Psychologist,* 1972, **27,** 499-503.

Lindner, R. M., & Seliger, R. V. *Handbook of correctional psychology.* New
      York: Philosophical Library, 1947.

Misiak, H., & Sexton, V. A. *History of psychology: An overview.* New York:
      Grune and Stratton, 1966.

Munsterberg, H. *On the witness stand.* New York: S. S. McClure, 1907.

Murphy, G. *Historical introduction to modern psychology.* (Rev. ed.) New
      York: Harcourt, Brace, and Company, 1949.

Sutherland, E. H., & Cressey, D. R. *Principles of criminology.* (5th ed.)
      Philadelphia: Lippincott, 1955.

University Microfilms. *A bibliography of doctoral research on crime and law
      enforcement.* Ann Arbor: Xerox, 1972.

CHAPTER THREE

Adams, S. Interaction between individual interview therapy and treatment
      amenability in older youth authority wards. *Board of Corrections
      monograph number two.* Sacramento: Printing Division, Documents
      Section, July, 1961.

Aichorn, A. *Wayward youth..* New York: Viking, 1935.

Alexander, F., & Healy, W. *Roots of crime.* New York: Alfred E. Knopf,
      1935.

Alexander, F., & Staub, H. *The criminal, the judge, and the public.* Glencoe:
      The Free Press, 1956.

Argyle, M. A new approach to the classification of delinquents with implica-
      tions for treatment. *Board of Corrections monograph number two.*
      Sacramento: Printing Division, Documents Section, July, 1961.

Babst, D. V., Gottfredson, D. M., & Ballard, K. B., Jr. Comparison of multiple
      regression and configural analysis techniques for developing base expec-
      tancy tables. *Journal of Research in Crime and Delinquency,* 1968, **5,**
      72-80.

Bloch, H. A., & Flynn, F. T. *Delinquency.* New York: Random House, 1956.

Bonger, W. A. *Criminality and economic conditions.* New York: Agathon
      Press, 1967.

Brunswik, E. *Systematic and representative design of psychological exper-
      iments.* Berkeley: University of California Press, 1949.

Burgess, R. L., & Akers, R. L. A differential association-reinforcement theory
      of criminal behavior. *Social Problems,* 1966, **14,** 128-147.

Cloward, R. A., & Ohlin, L. E. *Delinquency and opportunity.* Glencoe: The
      Free Press, 1961.

Cohen, H. L., Filipczak, J. A., & Bis, J. S. CASE Project: Contingencies applicable to special education. Progress Report, August, 1965 (mimeo).

Conrad, J. P. *Crime and its correction: An international survey of attitudes and practices.* Berkeley: University of California Press, 1965.

Cormier, B. M., Kennedy, M., Sangowicz, J., & Trottier, M. Presentation of a basic classification for criminological work and research in criminality. *Canadian Journal of Corrections,* 1959, **1**, 21-34.

Cressey, D. R. The development of a theory: Differential association. In M. E. Wolfgang, L. Savitz, & N. Johnston (Eds.), *The sociology of crime and delinquency.* New York: John Wiley and Sons, 1962.

Cronbach, L. Two disciplines of scientific psychology. *The American Psychologist,* 1957, **12**, 671-684.

Doleschal, E. Criminal statistics: A review of the literature. *Information review of crime and delinquency.* New York: National Council on Crime and Delinquency, 1968.

Durkheim, E. *Rules of the sociological method.* Glencoe: The Free Press, 1956.

Erikson, E. H. *Childhood and society.* New York: Norton, 1950.

Erickson, M. L., & Empey, L. T. Class position, peers, and delinquency. *Sociology and Social Research,* 1965, **49**, 268-282.

Eysenck, H. J. (Ed.), *Behavior therapy and the neuroses.* New York: Pergamon, 1960.

Fildes, R. E., & Gottfredson, D. M. Cluster analysis in a parolee sample. *Journal of Research in Crime and Delinquency,* 1971, **8**, in press.

Gibbons, D. C., & Garrity, D. L. A preliminary typology of juvenile delinquents. Unpublished manuscript, 1958.

Glaser, D. Differential association and criminological prediction. *Social Problems,* 1960, **8**, 6-14.

Glaser, D. Prediction Tables as Accounting Devices for Judges and Parole Boards. *Crime and Delinquency,* 1962, **8**, 239-258.

Glaser, D. *Effectiveness of a prison and parole system.* Indianapolis: Bobbs-Merrill, 1964.

Gold, M., Principal Investigator. National Survey of Youth. National Institute of Mental Health project.

Gottfredson, D. M. The correctional agency challenge to behavioral science. Paper presented as part of the Symposium on the Role of Psychology in Social Agency Operations Research, California State Psychological Association, San Francisco, December, 1961.

Gottfredson, D. M. Assessment and prediction methods in crime and delinquency. *Task Force report: Juvenile delinquency and youth crime.* The President's Commission on Law Enforcement and Administration of Justice, Washington, D.C.: United States Government Printing Office, 1966. Pp. 171-187.

Gottfredson, D. M., Ballard, K. B., Jr., & Lane, L. *Association analysis in a prison sample and prediction of parole performance.* Vacaville, California: Institute for the Study of Crime and Delinquency, 1963.

Gottfredson, D. M., & Beverly, R. F. Development and operational use of prediction methods in correctional work. *Proceedings of the Social Statistics Section of the American Statistical Association.* Washington, D.C.: American Statistical Association, 1962.

Gough, H. G. Predicting job effectiveness among correctional officers. In *Report of the Eighth Annual Training Institute for Probation, Parole, and Institutional Staff.* Berkeley: University of California School of Social Welfare, 1956. Pp. 1-17.

Gough, H. G., Peterson, D. R. The identification and measurement of predispositional factors in crime and delinquency. *Journal of Consulting Psychology,* 1952, **16**, 207-212.

Grant, J. D. The offender as a correctional man-power resource. Paper presented at the First National Symposium on Law Enforcement Science and Technology. Chicago, Illinois: March, 1967.

Grant, J. D., & Grant, M. Q. A group dynamics approach to the treatment of nonconformists in the Navy. *Annals of American Academy of Political and Social Science,* 1959, **322**, 135-136.

Grant, M. Q. Interaction between kinds of treatments and kinds of delinquents. *Board of Corrections monograph number two.* Sacramento: Printing Divison, Documents Section, July, 1961.

Havel, J. *Special Intensive Parole Unit Phase IV: The parole outcome study.* Sacramento, California: Department of Corrections, Research Division, Research Report No. 13, September, 1965.

Healy, W., & Bronner, A. *New light on delinquency and its treatment.* New Haven: Institute of Human Relations, 1936.

Illinois State Training School for Boys, Treatment Committee. Report on diagnostic categories, 1953.

Jesness, C. Youth Center Research Project, comparison of two treatment methods: Transactional analysis and behavior modification. California Youth Authority, personal communication, 1972.

Jenkins, R. L., & Hewitt, L. Types of personality structure encountered in child guidance clinics. *American Journal of Orthopsychiatry,* 1944, **14**, 84-94.

Jones, M. *The therapeutic community.* New York: Basic Books, 1953.

Klein, M. W. Criminological theories as seen by a criminologist: An evaluative review of approaches to the causation of crime and delinquency. Los Angeles: Youth Studies Center, University of Southern California, 1967 (rnimeo).

Knight, M. *William James.* London: Whitefriars Press, Penguin Books, 1954.

Kretschmer, E. *Physique and character.* New York: Harcourt, Brace, 1925.

Lejins, P. P. Pragmatic etiology of delinquent behavior. In C. B. Vedder

(Ed.), *The juvenile delinquent.* New York: Doubleday, 1954.

Lemert, E. M. *Social pathology: A systematic approach to the theory of sociopathic behavior.* New York: McGraw-Hill, 1951.

Lentz, W. P. Delinquency as a stable role. *Social Work*, 1966, **11**, 66-70.

Mannheim, H., & Wilkins, L. T. *Prediction methods in relation to Borstal training.* London: Her Majesty's Stationery Office, 1955.

Maslow, A. *Motivation and personality.* New York: Harper, 1954.

McKee, J. M. The Draper Experiment: A programmed learning project. In G. D. Ofiesh, & W. C. Meierhenry (Eds.), *Trends in programmed instruction.* National Education Association, 1964.

Merton, R. K. *Social theory and social structure.* Glencoe: The Free Press, 1957.

Miller, W. B. Some characteristics of present day delinquency of relevance to educators. Paper presented at the meetings of the American Association of School Administrators, 1959.

Moos, R. H. A situational analysis of a therapeutic community milieu. *Journal of Abnormal Psychology*, 1968, **73**, 49-61.

National Council on Crime and Delinquency. Open Hearings in Juvenile Courts in Montana, November, 1964 (mimeo).

Ohlin, L. E. *Selection for parole: A manual of parole prediction.* New York: Russell Sage Foundation, 1951.

Patterson, G. R. In L. Ullman, & L. Krasner (Eds.), *Case studies in behavior modification.* New York: Holt, 1965. Pp. 279-285.

Pearl, A. Quality control in evaluative research of correctional programs. Paper presented at the Ninth National Institute on Crime and Delinquency, Seattle, July, 1962.

Peterson, D. R., Quay, H. C. & Cameron, G. R. Personality and background factors in juvenile delinquency as inferred from questionnaire responses. *Journal of Consulting Psychology*, 1959, **23**, 395-399.

President's Commission on Law Enforcement and Administration of Justice. *A challenge of crime in a free society.* Washington, D.C.: United States Government Printing Office, 1967.

Quay, H. Personality dimensions in delinquent males as inferred from the factor analysis of behavior ratings. *Journal of Research in Crime and Delinquency,* 1964, **1**, 33-37.

Reckless, W. C. *The crime problem.* New York: Appleton-Century-Crofts, 1950.

Reckless, W. C., Dinitz, S., & Kay, B. The self-component in potential delinquency and potential nondelinquency. *American Sociological Review*, 1957, **22**, 566-570.

Reckless, W. C., Dinitz, S., & Murray, E. Self concept as an insulator against delinquency. *American Sociological Review*, 1956, **21**, 744-746.

References

166 Redl, F. In Witmer & Kotinsky (Eds.), *New perspectives for research in juvenile delinquency*. Washington, D.C.: Children's Bureau Publication Number 356, 1956.

Salter, A. *Conditoned reflex therapy*. New York: Putnam, 1961.

Scarpitti, F. R., Murray, E., Dinitz, S., & Reckless, W. C. The good boy in a high delinquency area. In M. E. Wolfgang, L. Savitz, & N. Johnston (Eds.), *The sociology of crime and delinquency*. New York: John Wiley and Sons, 1962.

Schragg, C. A. Social types in a prison community. Unpublished MA thesis, University of Washington Library, 1944.

Schwartz, R. D., & Skolnick, J. H. Two studies of legal stigma. In H. S. Becker (Ed.), *The other side: Perspectives on deviance*. Glencoe: The Free Press, 1964. Pp. 103-117.

Schwitzgebel, R. *Street corner research: An experimental approach to the juvenile delinquent*. Cambridge, Massachusetts: Harvard University Press, 1964.

Shah, S. A. A behavioral conceptualization of the development of criminal behavior, therapeutic principles, and applications: A report to the President's Commission on Law Enforcement and the Administration of Justice. Chevy Chase, Maryland: Center for Studies of Crime and Delinquency, National Institute of Mental Health, September, 1966 (mimeo).

Sheldon, W. H. *The varieties of human physique*. New York: Harbor, 1940.

Sheldon, W. H. *The varieties of temperament*. New York: Harbor, 1942.

Short, J. F., Jr. Differential association with delinquent friends and delinquent behavior. *Pacific Sociological Review*, 1958, 1(1), 21-25.

Skinner, B. F. *Science and human behavior*. New York: Macmillan, 1953.

Slack, C. W. Experimenter-subject psychotherapy: A new method of introducing intensive office treatment for unreachable cases. *Mental Hygiene*, 1960, **44**, 238-256.

State of California, Department of the Youth Authority, Standard Nomenclature Committee. *Report of Committee on Standard Nomenclature*, 1958.

Sullivan, C., Grant, J. D., & Grant, M. Q. The development of interpersonal maturity: Application to delinquency. *Psychiatry*, 1956, **20**, 373-385.

Sutherland, E. H. *Principles of criminology*. (5th ed. rev. by D. Cressey) New York: J. B. Lippincott Co., 1955.

Sykes, G. M., & Matza, D. Techniques of neutralization: A theory of delinquency. *American Sociological Review*, 1957, **22**, 664-670.

Sykes, G. M. *The society of captives*. Princeton, New Jersey: Princeton University Press, 1958.

Tannenbaum, F. *Crime and the community*. Boston: Ginn and Co., 1938.

Thorne, G. L., Tharp, R. G., & Wetzel, R. J. *Federal Probation*, 1967, **31**,

21-27.

Tharp, R. G., & Wetzel, R. J. *Behavior modification in the natural environment.* New York: Academic Press, 1969.

Toch, H. *Violent men: An inquiry into the psychology of violence.* Chicago: Aldine, 1969.

Toch, H. Change through participation (and vice versa). *Journal of Research in Crime and Delinquency,* 1970, **7**, 198-206.

Venezia, P. S. Delinquency as a function of intrafamily relationships. *Journal of Research in Crime and Delinquency,* 1968, **5**, 148-173.

Voss, H. L. Differential association and reported delinquent behavior: A replication. *Social Problems,* 1964, **12**, 78-85.

Warren, M. Q. The case for differential treatment of delinquents. *Proceedings of the Ninth Annual Research Meeting.* Olympia, Washington: Department of Institutions, Division of Research, Research Report, 1969, **2**(2), 18-23.

Warren, M. Q. Classification of offenders as an aid to efficient management and effective treatment. *Journal of Criminal Law, Criminology and Police Science,* 1971, **62**, 239-258.

Wenk, E. A., Principal Investigator. The assessment of correctional climates. MH 16461, National Institute of Mental Health project, in progress.

Wilkins, L. T. What is prediction and is it necessary? In *Research and potential application of research in probation, parole, and delinquency prediction.* New York: Citizens' Committee for Children of New York, Research Center, New York School of Social Work, Columbia University 1961.

Wilkins, L. T., & Gottfredson, D. M. *Research, demonstration and social action.* Davis, Calif.: National Council on Crime and Delinquency Research Center, 1969. Pp. 156-168.

Wolpe, J. *Psychotherapy by reciprocal inhibition.* Stanford, California: Stanford University Press, 1958.

CHAPTER FOUR

American Friends Service Committee. *Struggle for justice.* New York: Hill and Wang, 1971.

Corsini, R. Functions of the prison psychologist. *Journal of Consulting Psychology,* 1945, **9**, 101-104.

Howard, J. M., & Sommers, R. H. Resisting institutional evil from within. In N. Sanford, C. Comstock & Associates, *Sanctions for evil.* San Francisco: Jossey-Bass, 1971.

Opton, E. M., Jr. It never happened and besides they deserved it. In N. Sanford, C. Comstock & Associates, *Sanctions for evil.* San Francisco: Jossey-Bass, 1971.

168 Menninger, K. *The crime of punishment.* New York: Viking, 1968.

CHAPTER SIX

Abrahamsen, D. *Who are the guilty?* New York: Rinehart, 1952.

Banay, R. Mental health in corrective institutions. *Proceedings, The American Prison Association.* New York: American Prison Association, 1941.

Barnes, H. E., & Teeters, N. *New horizons in criminology* (3rd ed.) Englewood Cliffs, N.J.: Prentice Hall, 1959.

Brodsky, S. L. Mental disease and mental ability. In S. L. Brodsky & N. E. Eggleston (Eds.), *The military prison: Theory, practice and research.* Carbondale, Ill.: Southern Illinois University Press, 1970. Pp. 145-151.

Brodsky, S. L. Prisoners with promise. *Corrections Quarterly,* 1972, **2**(1), 16-26.

Bromberg, W., & Thompson, C. B. The relation of psychoses, mental defect, and personality to crime. *Journal of Criminal Law,* 1937, **28**, 70-89.

Dohrenwend, B. P., & Dohrenwend, B. S. The problem of validity in field studies of psychological disorder. *Journal of Abnormal Psychology,* 1965, **70**, 52-69.

Glueck, B. Concerning prisoners. *Mental Hygiene,* 1918, **2**, 178.

Karpman, B. Criminality, insanity and the law. *Journal of Criminal Law and Criminology,* 1949, **39**, 584-605.

Laing, R. D. *Knots.* New York: Pantheon, 1970.

Lindner, R. M. *The fifty-minute hour: A collection of true psychoanalytic tales.* New York: Rinehart, 1955.

Overholser, W. The Briggs Law in Massachusetts. *Journal of Criminal Law,* 1935, **25**, 859.

Poindexter, W. R. Mental illness in a state penitentiary. *Journal of Criminal Law, Criminology and Police Science,* 1955, **45**, 559-564.

President's Commission on Law Enforcement and Administration of Justice. *Task Force report: Corrections.* Washington, D.C.: U.S. Government Printing Office, 1967.

Roebuck, J. *Criminal typology.* Springfield, Ill.: Thomas, 1967.

Schlessinger, N., & Blau, D. A psychiatric study of a retraining command. *U.S. Armed Forces Medical Journal,* 1957, **8**, 397-405.

Schuessler, K. F., & Cressey, D. B. Personality characteristics of criminals. *American Journal of Sociology,* 1950, **56**, 476-484.

Schands, H. C. A report on an investigation of psychiatric problems in felons in the North Carolina Prison System. Chapel Hill, N.C.: Department of Psychiatry, University of North Carolina, 1958.

Schilder, P. The cure of criminals and prevention of crime. *Journal of Criminal Psychopathology,* 1940, **2**, 152.

Srole, L., Langner, T. S., Michael, S. T., Opler, M. K., & Rennie, T. A. C.

New York: McGraw-Hill, 1962.

Tappan, P. W. *Crime, justice and correction.* New York: McGraw-Hill, 1960.

Twomey, J. J. Offender diagnoses at the Diagnostic Depot, Illinois State Penitentiary, Menard, Illinois. Privately distributed report, 1967.

Vintner, R., & Janowitz, M. Effective institutions for juvenile delinquents: A research statement. *Social Service Review,* 1959, **33**, 118-130.

Waldo, G., & Dinitz, S. Personality characteristics of criminals, *Journal of Research in Crime and Delinquency,* 1967, **3**, 1-20.

Wilson, D. P. *My six convicts: A psychologist's three years in Fort Leavenworth.* New York: Rinehart, 1951.

CHAPTER SEVEN

Bandura, A. *Principles of behavior modification.* New York: Holt, Rinehart and Winston, 1969.

Bishop, C. H., & Blanchard, E. B. *Behavior therapy: A guide to correctional administration and programming.* Athens, Ga.: Institute of Government, University of Georgia, 1971.

Burchard, J., & Tyler, V. The modification of delinquent behavior through operant conditioning. *Behavior Research and Therapy,* 1965, **3**, 245-250.

Clements, C. B., & McKee, J. M. Programmed instruction for institutionalized offenders: Contingency management and performance contracts. *Psychological Reports,* 1968, **22**, 957-964.

Cohen, H. L., & Filipczak, J. *A new learning environment.* Washington, D.C.: Jossey-Bass Inc., 1971.

Cohen, H. L., Goldiamond, I., Filipczak, J., & Pooley, R. *Training professionals in procedures for the establishment of educational environments.* Silver Spring, Maryland: Educational Facility Press—IBR, 1968.

DeRisi, W. J. Performance contingent parole: A behavior modification system for juvenile offenders. Paper presented to American Psychological Association Convention, Washington, D.C., September, 1971.

Fineman, K. An operant conditioning program in a juvenile detention facility. *Psychological Reports,* 1968, **22**, 1,119-1,120.

Horton, L. Generalization of aggressive behavior in adolescent delinquent boys. *Journal of Applied Behavior Analysis,* 1970, **3**, 205-211.

Ingram, G. L., Gerard, R. E., Levinson, R. B., & Quay, H. C. An experimental program for the psychopathic delinquent: Looking into the correctional wastebasket. *Journal of Research in Crime and Delinquency,* 1970, **7**, 24-30.

Jesness, C. F. The Youth Center Research Project: Differential treatment of delinquents in institutions. American Justice Institute and California Youth Authority, Third Annual Progress Report to the National

References

170   Institute of Mental Health, December, 1970.

Levinson, R. B., Ingram, G. L., & Azcarete, E. "Aversive" group therapy: Sometimes good medicine tastes bad. *Crime and Delinquency*, 1968, **14**, 330-339.

Lewin, K.   *A dynamic theory of personality: Selected papers.* New York: McGraw-Hill, 1935.

McKee, J. M. Draper experiments in behavior modification. Paper presented at the Behavior Modification Institute, Tuscaloosa, Ala., May, 1969.

Patterson, G. R., Cobb, J. A., & Ray, R. S. A social engineering technology for retraining the families of aggressive boys. In H. Adams and L. Unikal (Eds.), *Georgia Symposium in Experimental Clinical Psychology.* Vol. II. Springfield, Ill.: Thomas, 1972.

Phillips, G. L., Fixsen, D. L., Phillips, E. A., & Wolf, M. M. Achievement place: Modification of the behaviors of pre-delinquent boys within a token economy. *Journal of Applied Behavior Analysis,* 1971, **4**, 45-49.

Schwitzgebel, R. Short-term operant conditioning of adolescent offenders on socially relevant variables. *Journal of Abnormal Psychology,* 1967, **71**, 134-142.

Schwitzgebel, R., & Covey, T. H. Experimental interviewing of youthful offenders within a church setting. *Journal of Clinical Psychology,* 1963, **19**, 487-488.

Skinner, B. F. *Science and human behavior.* New York: Macmillan, 1953.

Street, D., Vintner, R. D., & Perrow, C. *Organization for treatment. A comparative study of institutions for delinquency.* New York: Free Press, 1966.

Tyler, V. Application of operant token reinforcement to academic performance of an institutionalized delinquent. *Psychological Reports,* 1967, **21**, 249-260.

Tyler, V. & Brown, G. The use of swift, brief isolation as a group control device for institutionalized delinquents. *Behavior Research and Therapy,* 1965, **5**, 1-9.

Von Holden, M. H. A behavioral modification approach to disciplinary segregation. Paper presented to 99th Congress of Corrections, Minneapolis, Minn., Aug., 1969.

Zimbardo, P. G. The psychological power and pathology of imprisonment. Hearings before Subcommittee No. 3, House Committee on the Judiciary, 92nd Congress, Part II, Serial No. 15, Oct. 25, 1971, 152-157.

CHAPTER EIGHT

Abrahamsen, D. *The psychology of crime.* New York: Science Editions, 1960.

Bazelon, D. L. Implementing the right to treatment. *University of Chicago*

Law Review, 1969, **36,** 742-754.

Boslow, H. M., Rosenthal, D., Kandel, A., & Manne, S. H. Methods and experiences in group treatment of defective delinquents in Maryland. *Journal of Social Therapy,* 1961, **7,** (2).

Broder, G. J. Multidisciplinary approach to prisoner rehabilitation. In S. L. Brodsky & N. E. Eggleston (Eds.), *The military prison: Theory, research, and practice.* Carbondale, Illinois: Southern Illinois University Press, 1970.

Clements, C., & McKee, J. M. Programmed instruction for institutionalized offenders. *Psychological Reports,* 1968, **22,** 957-964.

Davis, A. J. Sexual assault in the Philadelphia prison system. In S. E. Wallace (Ed.), *Total institutions.* Chicago: Aldine, 1971.

Ethical standards for psychological research. *APA Monitor,* 1971, **2** (7), 9-28.

Gerard, R. E., Quay, H. D., & Levinson, R. B. *Differential treatment: A way to begin.* Washington, D.C.: Bureau of Prisons, 1970.

Hodges, E. F. Crime prevention by the Indeterminate Sentence Law. *American Journal of Psychiatry,* 1971, **128,** 291-295.

Jones, M. *The therapeutic community.* New York: Basic Books, 1953.

Kim, L. I. C. Personal communication, June 1972.

Levinson, R. B. 10 Year Plan, Mental Health Programs. Mental Health Memo, 12-72, Federal Bureau of Prisons, March 31, 1972.

Morris, N., & Hawkins, G. *The honest politician's guide to crime control.* Chicago: University of Chicago Press, 1970.

Pacht, A. Key issue study: How can clinical treatment programs for offenders be expanded and/or made more effective? Wisconsin Division of Corrections, June 1, 1972.

Parker, T. *The frying pan: A prison and its prisoners.* New York: Harper and Row, 1970.

President's Commission on Law Enforcement and the Administration of Justice. *Task Force report: Corrections.* Washington, D.C.: U.S. Government Printing Office, 1967.

Quay, H. E. Patterns of aggression, withdrawal, and immaturity. In H. C. Quay & J. S. Werry (Eds.), *Psychopathological disorders of childhood.* New York: Wiley & Sons, 1972.

Sturup, G. *Treating the untreatables.* Baltimore: Johns Hopkins University Press, 1968.

Warren, M. Q. Classification of offenders as an aid to efficient management and effective treatment. *Journal of Criminal Law, Criminology and Police Science,* 1971, **62,** 239-258.

Warren, M. Q. The case for differential treatment of delinquents. *Canadian Journal of Corrections,* 1970, **12**(4).

172 **CHAPTER NINE**

Allen, R. C., Ferster, E. Z., & Rubin, J. G. *Readings in law and psychiatry.* Baltimore, Md.: Johns Hopkins University Press, 1968.

Arens, R., & Meadow, A. Psycholinguistics and the confession dliemma. *Columbia Law Review*, 1956, **56**, 38-46.

Blumberg, A. *Criminal justice.* Chicago: Quadrangle, 1967.

Brodsky, S. L., & Robey. A. On becoming an expert witness. *Professional Psychology,* 1972, **3**, 173-176.

Carter, R., & Wilkins, L. *Probation and parole.* N. Y.: Wiley, 1970.

Cooke, G., & Jackson, N. L. P. Competence to stand trial: Role of the psychologist. *Professional Psychology*, 1971, **2**, 373-376.

Dreher, R. H. Origin, development and present status of insanity as a defense to criminal responsibility in the Common Law. *Journal of the History of the Behavioral Sciences*, 1967, **3**, 47-57.

Goldstein, A. *The insanity defense.* New Haven: Yale University Press, 1967.

Haward, L. R. C. Psychological experiment and judicial doubt. Bulletin of the British Psychological Society, 1964, **17**, 5A.

Haward, L. R. C. The psychologist in English criminal law. *Journal of Forensic Psychology*, 1969, **1**, 11-22.

Haward, L. R. C. The role of the psychologist in English criminal law. *Journal of Forensic Psychology*, 1971, **3**, 4-11.

Mode, E. B. Probability and criminalistics. *Journal of the American Statistical Association*, 1963, **58**, 628-640.

Mohr, J. W. The pedophilias: Their clinical, social and legal implications. *Canadian Psychiatric Association Journal*, 1962, **7**, 255-260.

Mohr, J. W., Turner, R. E., & Ball, R. B. Exhibitionism and pedophilia. *Corrective Psychiatry and Journal of Social Therapy*, 1962, **8**.

Padawer-Singer, A. Free Press, Fair Trial. Paper presented at the American Psychological Association Convention, Miami Beach, Florida, 1970.

Robey, A., & Brodsky, S. L. A bill of rights for the forensic psychiatrist. Paper presented at the meetings of the American Psychiatric Association, Dallas, Texas, May, 1972.

Sardoff, R. L. Mental illness and the criminal process: The role of the psychiatrist. *American Bar Association Journal*, 1968, **54**, 566-569.

Simon, R. J. *The sociology of law: Interdisciplinary readings.* San Francisco: Chandler, 1968.

Sugarman, A. G. (Ed.), *Examining the medical expert: Lectures and trial demonstrations.* Ann Arbor, Michigan: Legal-Medical Library, Institute of Continuing Education, 1969.

Ziskin, J. *Coping with psychiatric and psychology testimony.* Beverly Hills, Calif.: Law and Psychology Press, 1970.

Bard, M. Family intervention police teams as a community mental health resource. *Journal of Criminal Law, Criminology, and Police Science.* 1969, **60**, 247-250.

Bard, M. Training police as specialists in family crisis intervention. Washington, D.C.: U.S. Government Printing Office (and U.S. Dept. of Justice), 1970.

Barocas, H.A. A technique for training police in crisis intervention. *Psychotherapy: Theory, Research and Practice*, 1971, **8**, 342-343.

Blum, R. H. *Police selection.* Springfield, Ill.: Thomas, 1964.

Brussel, J. A. *Casebook of a crime psychiatrist.* New York: Dell, 1968.

Burger, K. (Ed.) *Mental illness and law enforcement.* St. Louis: Washington University Social Science Institute, 1970.

Danish, S. J. & Brodsky, S. L. Training of policemen in emotional control and awareness. *American Psychologist*, 1970, **25**, 368-369.

Ferguson, R. F. Creativity in law enforcement: The Covina field experiment. San Diego: Institute of Public and Urban Affairs, San Diego State College, 1970.

Gottesman, J. Personality patterns of urban police applicants as measured by by the MMPI. Hoboken, N.J.: Stevens Institute of Technology, 1969.

Marshall, J. *Law and psychology in conflict.* New York: Bobbs-Merrill, 1966.

Metropolitan Police Department, St. Louis, Missouri. Team counseling of hard-core delinquents. November, 1971.

Mills, R. B. Innovations in police selection and training. Paper presented at the Annual Convention of the American Psychological Association, San Francisco, September, 1968.

Narrol, H. G. & Levitt, E. E. Formal assessment procedures in police selection. *Psychological Reports*, 1963, **12**, 691-693.

Newman, L. E. & Steinberg, J. L. Consultation with police on human relations training. *American Journal of Psychiatry*, 1970, **126**, 1,421-1,429.

President's Commission on Law Enforcement and Administration of Justice. *Task Force report: The police.* Washington, D.C.: U.S. Government Printing Office, 1967.

Reiser, M. *The police department psychologist.* Springfield, Ill.: Thomas, 1972.

Rubin, R. *Stress training: Trainer's guide to police experience series.* New York: Film Modules, Inc., 1970.

Shellow, R. Active participation in police decision-making. Paper presented at the Annual Convention of the American Psychological Association, Washington, D.C., 1971.

Siegel, A. I., Federman, P. J., & Schultz, D. G. *Professional police—Human relations training.* Springfield, Ill.: Thomas, 1963.

174   Sikes, M. P., & Cleveland, S. E. Human relations training for police and community. *American Psychologist*, 1968, **23**, 766-769.

Smith, D. H. Police officer selection: A critical literature review. Paper presented at the Western Psychological Association Meetings, San Francisco, April, 1971.

Verinis, J. S., & Walker, V. Policemen and the recall of criminal details. *Journal of Social Psychology*, 1970, **81**, 217-221.

Wetteroth, W. J. The psychological training and education of New York City policemen. Paper presented at the Annual Convention of the American Psychological Association, Washington, D.C., 1971.

CHAPTER ELEVEN

Baehr, M. E., Saunders, D. R., Froemel, E. C., & Furcon, J. E. The prediction of performance for black and white police patrolmen. *Professional Psychology*, 1971, **2**, (1).

Megargee, E. I. The role of inhibition in the assessment and understanding of violence. In J. L. Singer (Ed.), *The control of aggression and violence*. N.Y.: Academic Press, 1971.

Singer, J. L. (Ed.), *The control of aggression and violence*. N.Y.: Academic Press, 1971.

Skelton, W. D. Prison riot: Assaulters vs. defenders. *Archives of General Psychiatry*, 1969, **21**.

Sokol, R. J., & Reiser, M. Training police sergeants in early signs of emotional upset. *Mental Hygiene*, 1971, **35** (3).

Sommer, R. Research priorities in correctional architecture. Final report submitted to the Law Enforcement Assistance Administration, U.S. Department of Justice, 1971.

Sterling, J. *Changes in role concepts of police officers*. Gaithersburg, Maryland: International Association of Chiefs of Police, 1972.

Toch, H. H. *Violent men*. Chicago: Aldine, 1969.

CHAPTER TWELVE

Heisler, G. H., & Brodsky, S. L. Graduate education in correctional psychology. Report prepared for the American Association of Correctional Psychologists, August, 1971.

Hoch, E. L., Ross, A. O., & Winder, C. L. *Professional preparation of clinical psychologists*. (Proceedings of the Conference on the Professional Preparation of Clinical Psychologists meeting at the Center for Continuing Education, Chicago, Ill., Aug. 27-Sept. 1, 1965.) Washington, D.C.: American Psychological Association, 1966.

Leonard, J. Announcement of the establishment of the Center for Correctional

Psychology. Tuscaloosa, Alabama, October 3, 1971.

Raimey, V. C. (Ed.) *Training in clinical psychology*. New York: Prentice-Hall, 1950.

Strother, C. R. (Ed.) *Psychology and mental health:* A report on the institute on education and training for psychological contributions to mental health, held at Stanford University in August, 1955. Washington, D.C.: American Psychological Association, 1956.

CHAPTER THIRTEEN

Department of Youth Services, Commonwealth of Massachusetts. Programs and policies of the Department of Youth Services. Mimeographed report, February, 1972.

Gottfredson, D. M. The base expectancy approach. In M. E. Wolfgang, L. Savitz, & N. Johnston (Eds.), *The sociology of punishment and correction*. New York: Wiley, 1970.

Interdepartmental Council to Coordinate all Federal Juvenile Delinquency Programs. Proposed national policy objectives in the juvenile delinquency-youth development area. Washington, D.C.: May, 1972.

Margolin, J. reported in Hampton, B. Three views on the role of psychologists in public policy making. *Professional Psychology*, 1970, **1**, 473-476.

Miller, D. K. Social reform and organized psychology. *Journal of Social Issues,* 1972, **28**, 217-231.

Morris, N., & Hawkins, G. *The honest politician's guide to crime control*. Chicago: University of Chicago Press, 1970.

Rieff, R. Psychology and public policy. *Professional Psychology,* 1970, **1**, 315-324.

Sellin, T., Wolfgang, M. E., & Figlio, R. *Delinquency in a birth cohort*. Chicago: University of Chicago Press, 1972.

Simon, L. J. The political unconscious of psychology: Clinical Psychology and social change. *Professional Psychology*, 1970, **1**, 331-341.

Skinner, B. F. *Beyond freedom and dignity*. New York: Knopf, 1971.

Thornberry, T. P. Punishment and Crime: The effect of legal dispositions on subsequent criminal behavior. Unpublished doctoral dissertation, University of Pennsylvania, 1971.

Warren, M. Q. The community treatment project: History and prospects. *Law Enforcement Science and Technology*, 1967, **1**, 191-200.

Wolfgang, M. E. Post-juvenile delinquency of a birth cohort. Summary of NIMH grant No. R01 13664, Philadelphia, 1971.

Zimring, F. Perspectives on deterrence. Washington, D.C.: NIMH Crime and

Delinquency Monograph, U.S. Government Printing Office, 1970.

CHAPTER FOURTEEN

Crary, W. E., & Steger, H. E. Prescriptive and consultative approaches to psychological evaluation. *Professional Psychology*, 1972, **3**, 105-110.

Hunt, R. C., & Wiley, E. D. Operation Baxstrom after one year. *American Journal of Psychiatry*, 1968, **124**, 974-978.

Jacobson, J. L., & Wirt, R. D. MMPI profiles associated with outcomes of group psychotherapy with prisoners. In J. N. Butcher (Ed.), *MMPI: Research developments and clinical applications.* New York: McGraw-Hill, 1969.

Kassebaum, G., Ward, D., & Wilner, D. *Prison treatment and parole survival: An empirical assessment.* New York: Wiley, 1971.

Kittrie, N. N. *The right to be different: Deviance and enforced therapy.* Baltimore: The Johns Hopkins Press, 1971.

Rollin, H. R. *The mentally abnormal offender and the law.* Oxford: Pergamon, 1969.

Sarbin, T. The dangerous individual: An outcome of social identity transformations. *British Journal of Criminology*, 1967, **22**, 285-295.

Index